CW00689293

Whitehills Through The Years
An Illustrated History
Including Boyndie, Boyne, and Ladysbridge.

Old Willie Levenie making a creel at Whitehills.

Former United Free Church Manse, No. 3 Seafield Street, Whitehills.
(Early 1900's).

2010 Banffshire Maritime & Heritage Association Committee Members:

Stanley Bruce	Chairman
Rosemary Sanderson	Vice-Chair
Jean Langham	Treasurer
S. Bruce / R. Sanderson	Joint Secretary
Liam Sparke	Committee
Nick Dolphin	Committee
Roger Lewendon	Committee
Malcolm Smith	Committee

Whitehills Through The Years
An Illustrated History
Including Boyndie, Boyne, and Ladysbridge.

By
Stanley Bruce

Published by
BARD BOOKS
On behalf of the
Banffshire Maritime & Heritage Association

♦ Whitehills Through the Years ♦

© Copyright – Stanley Bruce 2010.

First Edition.

ISBN 978-1-907234-04-0.

This edition published in 2010 by Bard Books.

All proceeds from the sale of this book will be donated to the Banffshire Maritime & Heritage Association. Registered Charity Number SCO40505.

www.banffshiremaritime.org.uk

Printed by Peters Design and Print, Turriff. Tel. 01888 563589

Contents   Page

Seafield Arms Hotel, No. 5 Chapel Street c1900.
(Courtesy Isobel Watt).

Introduction

This book gives a historical view of the village of Whitehills 'Throug the Years'. It also includes Ladysbridge, Boyndie, and Boyne, which ar all situated in the Parish of Boyndie.

The Parish of Boyndie lies on the Moray Firth coast, and is bounded o the east by the Parish of Banff and the Burn of Boyndie, which passe through the site of the now ruinous Banff Distillery. To the west it bounded by the Parish of Fordyce and the Burn of Boyne, which lie immediately west of the ruins of Boyne Castle, and to the south bounded by the Parish's of Ordiquhill (Cornhill) and Marnoc (Aberchirder).

Boyne in Irish Gaelic is 'Bóinne', which means stream and ford. Th name Banff is also thought to come from Irish Gaelic 'Banbh', whic means pig. A Banff seal dated 1408 clearly shows a pig as its mai feature, it is likely that the names of Boyne and Banff were bot established c600 by Irish settlers. The name Boyndie is thought to be diminutive (Smaller version) of Boyne, and Inverboyndie simply mear the 'Mouth of the Boyndie'.

The patron saint of the Parish is St. Brendan (Brandon) (d.1003). He remembered with associated names in the Parish as follows: The far of Brangan (Grid Ref NJ613648), St. Brandon's Stones (Grid R NJ607611), and St. Brandon's Church at Boyndie. Due south of Culle on Clune Hill there was once a small settlement, now lost, known Pittenbringan, (Grid Ref NJ515644).

Boyn (Bouyn), anciently gave name to two feudal territories, one th 'Thandedom of Boyn', and the other the 'Forest of Boyn'. Th Thanedom included the chief part of the Parish of Boyndie, and certa parts of Fordyce and Banff. The Forest of Boyn, lay to the east and we of the Bin of Cullen, and occupied a large extent of the south and east the Parish of Fordyce.

In the time of King Robert the Bruce (1274 to 1329) the Thanedom Boyn belonged to Thomas Randolph (d.1332) 1st Earl of Moray, ar Regent of Scotland. In 1313, during the Scottish Wars of Independen he recovered Edinburgh Castle from the English. In 1346 John Randolph (b.1306) 3rd Earl of Moray died with no heir, and his sister Agnes Randolph (Black Agnes) assumed the title Countess of Moray. On her death in 1369, King David II granted the Thanedom of Boyn to Sir John Edmonstone (d.1380's). The land came to the Ogilvie's c1486 through the marriage of Sir Walter Ogilvie (1460 to 1508) to Margaret Edmonstone daughter of Sir James Edmonstone (d.1486).

Knock Head, off which lie the Saut Stanes (Salt Stones) the location of many a shipwreck, is traditionally referred to as the location where the grey rat was first imported into Scotland from a vessel wrecked on the rocks. Three or four rats were found killing a litter of six piglets.

Whitehills was the last place in Scotland where fishermen sold their catch direct rather than deal through a fish merchant. However due to changes in the fishing industry the harbour and fish market became unviable, and since 2000 has been a very successful marina.

Whitehills today is a smashing, well-kept village, which in recent years has won the title 'Community of the Year'. The village is now reaping the benefits of the recently built wind farm, with considerable sums of money being injected into the community via Whitehills and District Community Council. The future of the community of Whitehills looks bright, and I am confident that folk will continue to love living here, and others will love coming to visit.

When I had the idea to write this book, I imagined a book with around 56 pages and 10,000 words, I am happy to say I was surprised with the amount of history in and around Whitehills and we have a book of 88 pages and over 17,500 words. I hope you are also surprised and I very much hope you enjoy it.

A' the best,

Stanley A. Bruce, BSc; I.Eng., IMarEng., MIMarEST,
Chairman, Banffshire Maritime & Heritage Association.

Whitehills Through the Years.

c2000BC St. Brandon's (St. Brannan's) stone circle was erected. It is thought to have been oval measuring 28 feet by 19 feet. Its remains stand near the farm of Templeton, which in the sense of a Druid Temple obviously takes its name from the circle. All that remains today are two upright stones, both of grey granite. The western stone is said to have twelve cup-marks, as recorded by Dr. Black in 1866, however due to a build up of earth and weeds most of these cannot be seen (Eight

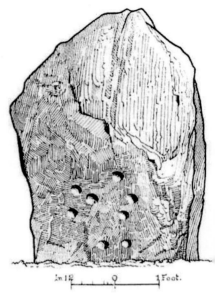

St. Brandon's c1900 sketch of the cup-marked stone. (Fred Coles).

were visible in 1900 when Fred Coles did his sketch). The base of the west stone is said to have two cup-marks near it base. The recumbent stone (Removed in the 1960's) is sai to have been eight feet long. (St. Brandon was an Irish mon who later became an Abbot and died in **1003**). According t William Cramond in 1886, one stone was six feet high b three feet wide and the other five feet high. *See* **1845**. Gri Ref NJ60756105.

c2000BC In the Parish of Boyndie stood a further two stone circles:

1) At St. Brandon's Parish Church of **1773**, close to the sout wall Grid Ref NJ642638. (Nothing visible today). At th site it is also recorded that a huge red stone stood near th manse offices and that a stone coffin was found, but thes

two items are both now lost.

2) 1 mile northeast of St. Brandon's Church, approximate Grid Ref NJ6564. (Nothing visible today).

1000 to 700BC   A sword (Broken in two) of this date was found at the Boar's Moss, Blairshinnoch, Boyndie in *1842*, it is now kept in Elgin Museum. Another leaf shaped sword was found here, and along with two others which were given to Banff Museum. Grid Ref NJ640622. See *1945*.

Late Bronze Age sword found at the Boar's Moss, Boyndie, in 1842, 645mm long by 37mm wide blade with by 56mm maximum width. (Elgin Museum).

83 to 138   The Red Well (Locally pronounced Reed Waal) is said to have been built by the Romans. The Romans won a great battle against the Picts at Mons Grapius in 83 or 84 AD. This battle occurred somewhere in the north east of Scotland. The Romans later retreated to the Antonine Wall c138AD. Therefore, if the Red Well was built by the Romans it would have been built between these dates. A strange phenomenon regarding the well is that during the sunrise of the Autumn Equinox a ray of light illuminates the inside of the well while the outside is still in darkness. The well is a chalybeate spring, which appears red due to the iron salt content, hence the name. The well was once very popular with people 'Taking the waters' for medicinal purposes. It is said that the well is haunted by an old woman wearing black. On New Years Day *1990*, sixteen-year old Christopher Christie of Whitehills stated that he was chased by a ghost who several times passed straight through him, and then followed him home and tried to steal his breath during the night. When these wells were built, they often had keepers who maintained and looked after them. The old woman may have

been the ghost of a former keeper. For a short while the well ha
a mannequin inside dressed as a Roman, which was a nic
feature, however it mysteriously caught fire. The well now has
rather out of character galvanised gate fitted (Not shown
Surprisingly the well is not currently listed, nor is it a Schedule
Ancient Monument. Grid Ref NJ662654.

Sign at the Red Well.

The Red Well, Boyndie Bay. (S. Bruce).

c1000 A battle took place at Banff Links near Inverboyndie, when th
Scots fought and defeated a band of invading Danish Viking
This battle is remembered with the names Arrdanes (Dane
with arrows) west of the Boyndie Burn, and Swordanes (Dane
with swords) east of the Boyndie Burn. In a field across th
road from Inverboyndie Kirk, approximately 30 yards north i
said to be where the dead Vikings were buried in a large pi
(Kenneth III was King of Scots from 997 to 1005).

c1000 A rubble built circular structure at Inverboyndie recorded on the map of 1902 as a well, (St. Brandon's Well?) may have been built around this date. Today this structure stands

Inverboyndie Well. (S. Bruce).

approximately four feet high, and can only be seen in the winter months when the weeds die down. If it is not saved soon it will be lost forever. Grid Ref NJ666643. Currently it does not appear to be listed.

1003 St. Brandon who was a Benedictine Monk died. His festival is the 16th May, and he is said to have been a good friend of King Malcolm II (d.1034) prior to him becoming king. Brannan Fair, a feeing market, was held annually at Brannan Howe near Inverboyndie Kirk on the 16th May. It was later held in Old Market Place, Banff.

c11th/12th C Two items from this period have been found in the Parish of Boyndie. In 2004, at Grid Ref NJ6564 south of Whitehills a complete Viking copper-alloy polyhedral kidney-ringed pin, with shank bent at 90° and length 180mm was found, Treasure Trove Ref TT.89/04. In 2006, also at Grid Ref NJ6564 an 87.2mm long by 3mm diameter cast bronze pin with a spiral head, made by splitting the top of the pin and hammering it open then shaping the two split parts by flattening them into two spirals, Treasure Trove Ref TT.78/06. Both items were allocated to the Marischal Museum in Aberdeen. See *17th C* for another find.

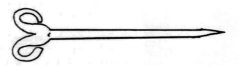

Sketch of the cast bronze pin (TT.78/06)

c1190   In an ancient Charter, King William the Lion (c1143 to 1214) William I of Scotland granted the Roman Catholic churches of Inverbondyn (Inverboyndie) and Banef (Banff) to the monks of Arbroath. He is traditionally credited with founding Arbroath Abbey. Inverboyndie Kirk was later confirmed to the monks of Arbroath by the following Bishops of Aberdeen: Mathew (1178 to 1199), John (1199 to 1207), Adam (1207 to 1228), Gilbert (1228 to 1239) and Ralph (1239 to 1247).

c1300   Craig of Boyne Castle was built. The builder is more than likely to have been one of the Comyn Earl's of Buchan, who at that time were the hereditary Sheriffs of Banffshire. This early fortification stood on the west side of the Burn of Boyne much nearer the sea than the ruined castle we see today, which was built *c1580*. This site was listed as an Ancient Scheduled Monument in 1992. Grid Ref NJ616663.
Cambridge County Geographies - Banffshire by W. Barclay, published in 1922 records a kitchen midden at the Craig of Boyne Castle, which was found to have relics dating as far back as mediaeval times. It records that one item was definitely dated from the fourteenth century.

13th C   Thomas Learmont, aka Thomas the Rhymer (c1220 to c1298) was a mediaeval Scottish seer who wrote prophetic verses, he wrote about St. Brandon's stones:

At two full times, and three half times,
Or threescore years and ten,
The ravens shall sit on the Stanes o' St. Brandon,
And drink o' the blood o' the slain!

14th C   At this time Boyne was spelt as Bouyn.

1369   7th March – In recognition of services rendered during the 2nd Wars of Scottish Independence (1332 to 1357) with England,

Sir John Edmonstone (d.1380's) received from King David II (d.1371) a grant of the Thanedom of Boyne.

14 /15th C   A silver 'Fede' ring of this date was found near Boyndie; it can currently be seen in Banff Museum. A 'Fede' ring is a mediaeval love or marriage ring and depicts two clasped hands signifying betrothal. The Boyndie ring is inscribed MARIA on one side, the other name is unclear.

Fede Ring.
(Banff Museum).

1458   The lands of Inverbundy (Inverboyndie) were leased to William Pyper by the Abbot and Convent of Arbroath. This included "The tithes of white fish, and the land and liberty of the brew house, for payment of £4 annually".

1484   From this date, there is a connection with the Ogilvie family and Culphin (Culfin) in Boyndie, through Walter Ogilvie of Auchleven. *See 1720.*

1484   Sir Walter Ogilvie (1460 to 1508) of Boyne married Margaret Edmonstone who was the daughter and heir of Sir James Edmonstone (d.1486).

1485   The Abbot of Arbroath granted to Sir James Ogilvie of Deskford the tithes (Obligation of supporting) of the churches of Banff and Inverbunde for payment of £44 annually.

c1486   Sir Walter Ogilvie (1460 to 1508) acquired the Thanedom of Boyne through marriage to Margaret Edmonstone daughter of Sir James Edmonstone (d.1486).

1498   The Abbot of Arbroath granted to Sir James Ogilvie of Deskford the tithes (Obligation of supporting) of the churches of Banff and Inverbunde for payment of £64 annually.

15th C   From this date, or perhaps even earlier, a small settlement of fisher folk lived at the mouth of the Boyndie Burn at Inverboyndie, approximately one mile to the east of Whitehills. This settlement was known as Knocmachair /Cnocmachair, Gaelic for round hill and grassy plain.

1559 Walter Ogilvie, second son of Sir Walter Qgilvie (1504 to 1561) 3rd Laird of Boyne, had a Charter of the Lands of Baldavie.

1560 William Cramond in 1886 recorded that the oldest tombstone in Inverboyndie Kirkyard was possibly as old as the Reformation (1560). He recorded that it was a small broken slab with the arms, two fetterlocks (A type of handcuff, an emblem of victory) over a mullet (A star), and the inscription 'Hic jacet honor', which means 'Here lies an honourable man'. (This stone I could not locate).

Mary, Queen of Scots c1559.

1562 19th September – Queen Mary of Scots (1542 to 1587) stayed at the Craig of Boyne Castle (Built *c1300*).

1564 Mary Beaton (Bethune) one of Mary, Queen of Scots' four Mary's, described as being pretty and plump, with fair hair, and dark eyes was courted by Thomas Randolph (1523 to 1590) who was 24 years her senior. Randolph at the time was the English Ambassador to the Scottish Court representing Queen Elizabeth I (1533 to 1603) of England, and he wanted Mary Beaton to spy on Queen Mary. She refused to be his spy, and called off their courtship and married Alexander Ogilvie of Boyne in *1566*.

1566 3rd May – Alexander Ogilvie (c1530 to c1606) 4th Laird of Boyne married Mary Beaton (Bethune) (1543 to 1598). Their marriage contract was signed by Mary, Queen of Scots (1542 to 1587), Henry Stuart (1545 to 1567) Lord Darnley, George Gordon (d.1576) 5th Earl of Huntly, Archibald Campbell (d.1573) 5th Earl of Argyle, James Hepburn (c1534 to 1578) 4th Earl of Bothwell, James Stuart (c1531 to 1570) 1st Earl of Murray (Moray), John Stewart, 4th Earl of Atholl (d.1579), and of course the bride and groom. Both the bride and groom are buried in Deskford Churchyard, near Cullen.

1575 The Boyne Estate was bought by Sir George Ogilvie (b.c1539) of Dunlugas.

1576 The Parishes of Inverbundye (Inverboyndie), Banff, and Alveth (Alvah) formed a single charge under minister Mr. William Lawtie (d.c1590) being separated from Fordyce.

c1580 Boyne Castle was built to supersede the earlier fortified building of *c1300*, which stood on the west side of the Burn of Boyne (Fordyce Parish), known as the 'Craig of Boyne Castle'. The new castle, is thought to have been wholly built by Sir George Ogilvie (b.c1539) of Dunlugas, who bought the estate in **1575**.

Boyne Castle as viewed from the west. (S. Bruce).

This castellated mansion with a ground plan of approximately 89 feet by 104 feet with a round 'drum' tower at all four corners was built on rising ground protected by the Boyne Burn to the west and partially to the north and south, and had a sunken moat at the east approximately fifty-five feet wide by ten feet deep. The castle gateway was via a raised roadway through the moat protected by two towers (Making six in total). It was in its day a truly magnificent building, with terraced gardens. Today however the gardens are overgrown, and the castle is in a very ruinous state, robbed of its charms. Category B listed. Boyne Castle was listed as a Scheduled Ancient Monument in *1933*. Grid Ref NJ612657. On the opposite bank of the Burn of Boyne is the *17th* C castle doo-cot.

1591 The Parish of Alveth (Alvah) was united with Forglen, but Inverbondy (Inverboyndie) and Banff remained together.

Early The Seatown of Whitehills is thought to have been in
1600's existence around this date. A small settlement certainly existed in *1634*.

1626   26th November (A Sunday) – the Minister of Inverboyndie Kirk recorded in the Book of Presbytery of the 'Horrible and barbarous miscarriage of some of his parishoners'. His sermon was interrupted and blood was shed during a feud between James Hockit of Cairntown and his son Jon. Hockit of Brangand against Peter Barklay of Whytnie. Because of this incident the Minister was ordered to speak to the Bishop.

1631   15th April – Inverboyndie Kirk Book of Presbytery records that Rev. William Chalmers summoned Sir George Ogilvie of Banff, knight, baronet to stand before the church and explain the slaughter of James Ogilvie. The book does not record any outcome.

c1634   Inverboyndie Kirk was built on the site of an earlier kirk, which is mentioned in 1008 and *c1190*. It measures 80 feet by 26 feet internally. The original bell-cote is said to have had the initials 'ILF' carved on it, which are thought to be those of James Ogilvie (d.1652) 1st Lord (Earl) of Findlater. The bell-cote as seen today was erected in *1740*, and the bell in *1770*. Today only the western gable of the kirk stands. The kirkyard has several old gravestones some with symbols of mortality, and

Inverboyndie Kirk.
(S. Bruce).

some are of the recumbent table style. The kirk was abandoned in *1773* and a new church built nearer the centre of the Parish at Boyndie. A silver Communion Beaker of *1720* from the church (one of a pair) is on display in Banff Museum. The church is category B listed, and in 1993 was registered as a Scheduled Ancient Monument.

The low arched building on the north side of the kirk is said to have been the burying place of the Ogilvie's of Boyne. Grid Ref NJ667645. *See 1738, and Appendix E.*

Ancient arched building, Inverboyndie Kirk. (S. Bruce).

1635 17th June – Banff was separated from the Parish of Boyndie.

1641 Christian Ogilvie of Boyne, the only daughter of Walter Ogilvie of Boyne married Sir James Baird (d.1691) 5th Laird of Auchmedden and they lived fifty years together. Sir James was later the Provost of Banff 1646-7 and 1661-6. They are both buried in St. Drostan's Kirk, New Aberdour. In St. Drostan's there is a

Christian Ogilvie of Boyne, coat of arms on the Baird Memorial Panel (1659) St. Drostan's Kirk, New Aberdour. (S. Bruce).

badly weathered red sandstone monument erected by Sir James, possibly in 1659 to the memory of his predecessors, Andrew, George, Gilbert, and George Baird, whose ashes are here interred. They died respectively 10th Feb 1543, 29th May 1593, 23rd Feb 1620, and 12th Feb 1642. The ashes of Anne Fraser and Elizabeth Keith his mother and great-grandmother respectively likewise also lie here interred. Christian's weathered coat of arms and her initials 'C O' can still be seen on the monument. The shield is Ogilvie (Lion) quartered with Edmonstone (Three crescents). *See 1484, and 1485/6.*

1645 James Graham (1612 to 1650) 1st Marquess of Montrose is recorded as travelling from Findlater to Boyne, plundering and burning the lands of Boyne and Boyne Castle before moving on to do the same in Banff. Sir Walter Ogilvie (d.1671) 7th Laird of Boyne held fast in the old Craig of Boyne Castle.

1654 Blaeu's Atlas of this date refers to Buch-chragie (Buchragie). The Manor Place of Buchragie owned by the Ogilvie family was once a great house thought to have been built in mediaeval times, but today nothing remains. A large standing stone is said to have once stood at this location. Grid Ref NJ65896439.

Site of enclosures, standing stones, and Buchragie House (Grid Ref NJ659643). (1902 map).

17th C A silver brooch from this period was found at Inverboyndie. Treasure Trove Ref TT.62/04. The item was allocated to Aberdeenshire Heritage. See *11th/12th C* for other finds.

1656 The Minister of Inverboyndie Kirk was ordered to ensure a Schoolmaster was provided for the Parish.

1659 9th November – Mr. Alex Turner sometime of Kindrought gifted 1,000 merks for the poor and other pious uses within the Parish.

1660 The Book of Presbytery of Inverboyndie Kirk records that the Minister's house at Inverboyndie was ruinous.

c1662 Patrick Ogilvie (d.1714) of Boyne was knighted.

1674 October – Thomas Ruddiman (d.1757) was born at Raggal, Boyndie (Grid Ref NJ620618). His father James (c1640 to 1707) was a farmer and Elder of Inverboyndie Kirk. His mother was Margaret Simpson of Little Rettie. Thomas was one of six children. At the age of sixteen (October 1690), with a guinea in his pocket from his sister Agnes, he made his way to Aberdeen to compete for a bursary at Kings College. On route, he was robbed by gypsies who stripped him near naked and took his guinea. This, however, did not stop him winning the first bursary and he commenced his studies in November 1690. On 21st June 1694, he graduated with the degree Master of Arts (M.A.). Later he became the Schoolmaster at Laurencekirk.

In 1700, he was employed as an assistant librarian in the Advocates' Library, Edinburgh. In *1714*, he published his 'Rudiments of the Latin Tongue'. Thomas and his brother Walter established a printing business in Parliament Close, Edinburgh and founded the Caledonian Mercury Newspaper. In 1730, he was appointed chief librarian in the Advocates' Library, Edinburgh. Two of the notable works he edited were the valuable edition of Æneid by Bishop Gavin Douglas (1474 to 1522) published in 1710, and in 1715 the splendid two volume edition of historian George Buchanan (1506 to 1582). He died 19th January 1757, and is buried in Greyfriar's Churchyard, Edinburgh. *See 1794.*

1676 19th January – Mr. William Simsone (Described as a young man) was lawfully chosen by Sir Patrick Ogilvie (d.1714) 8th Laird of Boyne, and the Minister and the Session of Inverboyndie Kirk as the new Schoolmaster.

1678 The records of the Presbytery show that a new manse was being built for the Minister of Inverboyndie. *See 1660.*

1681 Sir Patrick Ogilvie (d.1714) 8th Laird of Boyne had a Royal Warrant which allowed him to hold two yearly markets in Boyndie, one in the Muir of Whitehills on the 2nd Tuesday of May, the other on the Muir of Culfin (Culphin) on 2nd Tuesday of October. The warrant also allowed for a weekly market to be held at Portsoy.

c17th C The doo-cot at Boyne Castle was built on the western side of the Burn of Boyne. Boyne Castle built *c1580* stands on the eastern side of the burn. The doo-cot has nesting boxes for approximately 750 pigeons.

Boyne Castle Doo-cot.
(S. Bruce).

It has crow-stepped gables and the usual rat-ledge. The roof has recently collapsed, so it is currently unsafe to access. Category B listed. Grid Ref NJ611657.

1685 20th April - Patrick Ogilvie (d.1714) 8th Laird of Boyne attended a Privy Council meeting and signed a declaration against the National Covenant of 1638 and the Solemne League and Covenant of 1643, declaring them both illegal.

1698-9 Between 13th November 1698 and 12th November 1699 fifteen men and fifteen women compeared (Appeared) before the Inverboyndie Kirk Session for breaches of the 7th Commandment (Thou Shalt Not Commit Adultery).

1701 Patrick Cook was the Schoolmaster at Inverboyndie.

1707 Sir James Ogilvie (1667 to *1727)* 9th Laird (Baron) of Boyne from *1714* opposed the Union of Parliaments.

1714 Thomas Ruddiman (*1674* to 1757) of Boyndie published his 'Rudiments of the Latin Tongue', which immediately superseded all other grammars in Scottish schools.

1714 Sir Patrick Ogilvie 8th Laird of Boyne died. He was succeeded by his son Sir James Ogilvie (1667 to *1727)* who became the 9th Laird of Boyne. *See **Appendix E**.*

1720 James Ogilvie of Culphin (Culfin) gave two silver Communion Beakers to Inverboyndie Kirk. The Beaker shown is currently on display in Banff Museum, and is engraved – 'JAMES OGILVIE OF CULPHIN DEDICATED 1720'. It is said that it was made by Scott, a silversmith of Banff. *See 1484.*

1720 Communion Beaker. (N. Dolphin).

1723 A carved stone of this date can be seen in a wall at Inverboyndie Kirk. The stone reads:

'LORD I HAVE LOVED THE HABITATION OF THY HOUSE AND THE PLACE WHERE THINE HONOUR DWEL LETH.
THIS ENTRY DOOR TO THE CHURCH WAS PUT UP BY ME JAMES OGILVIE OF CULPHIN WHO WAS AN ELDER AT THIS PLACE FOURTY SIX YEARS BY PAST AT THIS PRESENT YEAR OF GOD 1723'.

1723 carved stone Inverboyndie Kirk. (S. Bruce).

1727   James Ogilvie (b.1667) 9th Laird of Boyne died in Paris. James, fought on the side of the Jacobites at the Battle of Sheriffmuir in 1715, and was described as the 'Brigadier Ogilvie'. After the suppression of the Jacobite rising he remained in hiding in the north of Scotland before escaping to France.

1727   A hand-bell of this date which can be seen inside Whitehills Parish Church, Seafield Street, is inscribed 'The village of Whithills', (No 'e') and was used as the Town Crier's bell, as late as the 20th century. See *1860, and 1925-6.*

Town Crier's Bell, Whitehills Parish Church. (S. Bruce).

1730   The Parish Church Book of the Presbytery records that there were two Jacobite prelatical meeting houses on the confines of the Parish of Boyndie.

1731   The Ogilvie family of Boyne got into financial difficulties and sold the Boyne Estate to James Ogilvie (1688 to 1764) 5th Earl of Findlater and 2nd Earl of Seafield.

1733   An old chair made of fir bearing this date now in Whitehills Parish Church, Seafield Street, Whitehills, came from St. Brandon's Church at Boyndie, however it originally came from Inverboyndie Kirk. The chair also bears the initials 'IA' for James Anderson a former Minister of Inverboyndie Kirk. It was moved to Boyndie Parish

1733 chair Whitehills Parish Church. (S. Bruce).

Church in *1773*, and used by the Moderator at Kirk Session meetings.

1738   Date of the armorial tablet in the Inverboyndie Kirkyard (Built *c1634)*. The lair is to James Milne sometime at Mill of Boyndie and to his two sons John Milne also Mill of Boyndie (Grid Ref NJ664642) and Alexander Milne Mill of Alvah (Grid Ref NJ677608). The tablet was erected by James Milne, Nether Mill of Boyndie who was the eldest son of the second John Milne. See *1740*. Grid Ref NJ667645.

James Milne, Armorial Tablet, Inverboyndie Kirkyard. (S. Bruce).

1738   Elspeth Simpson (d.1791) was born at Rothmackenzie in Fordyce Parish. (Grid ref NJ579589). She was the daughter of John Simpson and Margaret Gordon, proprietor of an inn at Fatmacken (Fetney-Can) now known as Fitmacan, a halfway house between Banff and Portsoy Grid Ref NJ637645. Whilst working at Delftfield Pottery in Greenock she met Robert Buchan, a journeyman potter who she married 13th July 1760. The couple and their three children later moved to Banff where Mr. Buchan opened a small pottery, and Mrs. Buchan opened an infant school where she taught needlework and the rudiments of spelling. Mr. Buchan's business was not a success and he abandoned his wife and his children and headed for Glasgow. Elspeth continued to teach in Banff, but her fanatical religious beliefs estranged her, and her school became poorly attended. Around 1780 she decided to follow her husband and headed for Glasgow where they were reunited. In Glasgow, she met Rev. Hugh White and she convinced him that she was one of the figures in the Book of Revelation "The woman clothed with the sun". She later moved to Irvine to be near Rev. Hugh White. After being expelled from Irvine in 1783, she was the founder of a fanatical sect known as the Buchanites. Mrs. Buchan also claimed that she was immortal, and that she had the ability to make her followers immortal by breathing upon them. After her death in 1791, the fanatical sect continued until 1846.

Inverboyndie Kirk bellcote of 1740. (S. Bruce).

1740   A new Bellcote was erected at Inverboyndie Kirk. The corbelling below the bellcote on the gable wall of the kirk is thought to have supported an earlier bellcote, probably when the kirk was built in *c1634.* Category B listed, and a Scheduled Ancient Monument. See *1738.*

1741   The Inverboyndie Kirk Books of Presbytery record that a Whitehills fishing boat was lost at sea, and seven men perished, leaving five widows and eighteen fatherless children.

c1754   'Alternate Husbandry' was introduced by James Ogilvie (d.1770) later 6th Earl of Findlater and 3rd Earl of Seafield on the farm of Craigherbs, Boyndie, replacing the run-rig system. This was one of the first farms in the north of Scotland to adopt this modern method of farming. c1700, the agriculture of Scotland was still of the simplest kind. There were no dykes enclosing the land, and the livestock of each community grazed together in common land. Some farmers were still growing crops of white corn year after year on the same ground, until the ground was exhausted; and had to be left to nature to recover. Ogilvie introduced a much-improved system where turnips, clover, and ryegrass, were grown alternately with grain crops, hence the name 'Alternate Husbandry'. Working class folk grew potatoes in their gardens for their own use, but they were not yet grown in the fields. The building of the trunk roads greatly helped the farmers, who could now get lime to fertilise their fields, and get their crops to market more easily. Hedges were planted, ditches dug and fields drained. When Blackpots Brick & Tile Works was established *c1788,* field drains were greatly in demand.

1755   The population of Boyndie Parish was 994.

1757   19th January – James Ruddiman (b.1674) died. A memorial to him in Greyfriars Churchyard, Edinburgh reads "Thomas Ruddiman A.M sacred to the memory of that celebrated scholar and wirthy man, Thomas Ruddiman A.M., Keeper of the Advocates' Library near fifty years. Born October 1674, within three miles of the town of Banff; died in Edinburgh 19th January, 1757, in his eighty-third year'. The tablet was erected as a respectful tribute, by his relative, William Ruddiman M.D., 1801.

1762/3 Ogilvie of Culvie and his father were feuars of Baldavie, and they sold to James Ogilvie (1688 to 1764) 5th Earl of Findlater, and 2nd Earl of Seafield.

1770   A new bell made by Hugh Gordon of Aberdeen was fitted to the bellcote of Inverboyndie Kirk. This bell was stolen and its whereabouts is unknown. *See **1634**.*

Mid to The Inverboyndie Bridge over the Burn of Boyndie was built.
late   This is a double arch bridge, with each arch approximately
18th C thirteen feet long. Category B listed. Grid Ref NJ668645.

Double-arched road bridge at Inverboyndie. (S. Bruce).

Mid to late 18th C   The roof was removed from Boyne Castle and hewn stones were removed and reused in the build of new buildings in the Parish.

1773   St. Brandon's Church, Boyndie was built further inland and nearer the centre of the Parish than the earlier Parish Kirk at Inverboyndie of *c1634.* This was to better suit the members of the rural congregation. It had seats for 600, and originally had three galleries. The fishers of Whitehills had their own special gallery with its own entrance. It was extended in *1922,* and remained in use until *1996.* It was badly damaged by fire in *2000.* Category B listed. Grid Ref NJ642638.

18thC Boyndie lead communion token. Reads 'BOYN'. Left - St. Brandon's Church, Boyndie in 1996. (Photos I.Watt.).

c1775   A manse was built at Boyndie, however, it was replaced in *1841-2.*

1787   20th February – James Raeburn was born at Boyndie. Although his training as an architect is unrecorded, he, in 1827, became Principal Clerk of Works at the Scottish Office of Works in Edinburgh, a position he held until 1839. Amongst his work is the Music Hall, Aberdeen in 1820 (Category A listed), and the Banff Free Church (1843), later known as the Trinity and Alvah Church, Castle Street, Banff (Category B listed). He died 30th September 1851. His son Robert Reid Raeburn (1819 to 1888) followed in his footsteps.

Late 18th C   The single arch rubble built bridge over the Burn of Boyne at Scotsmill was built. The bridge span is approximately 20 feet.

Category B listed. Grid Ref NJ611654.

c1788 The Brick and Tile Works at Blackpots (A little east of Whitehills) was established by Alexander Saunders. Black clay was dug from Knock Head (100 feet high) and transported down to the factory on a small narrow gauge railway with small bogies pushed manually. The clay was then made into bricks, field drainage pipes and pan tiles for roofs.

Blackpots Brick and Tile Works. (Photographer unknown).

It is recorded that in one season the factory made 250,000 field drainage pipes. It is thought that the red bricks, used to construct the boundary wall at Duff House / Airlie Gardens in Banff were made at Blackpots. *See **1900, 1973, 1974,** and **1977.*** Grid Ref NJ659657.

Small bogie full of clay, Blackpots. (Photographer unknown).

1794 George Chalmers (1742 to 1825) wrote 'The life of Thomas Ruddiman, A. M.' The Keeper, for almost Fifty Years, of the Library belonging to the Faculty of Advocates at Edinburgh: to which are subjoined new anecdotes of Buchanan'. This is available to read online at www.books.google.com. *See 1674.*

1794   The house known as Greystones No. 22 Seafield Street was built. This building is thought to have once been an Inn with stables.

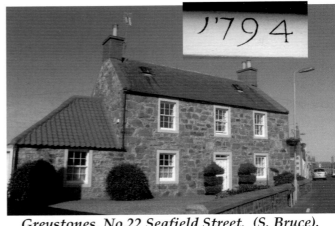

Greystones, No.22 Seafield Street. (S. Bruce).

(Perhaps rebuilt around an earlier building). It was also used as a tailors shop. Category B listed by Historic Scotland.

Late   Blackpots Harbour was built. The harbour pier and sea wall
18th C are both of rubble construction. The harbour was used by salmon fishermen for export of their catch mainly to London, and by the nearby Brick and Tile Works for export of their products. The salmon bothy stood directly south of the harbour, and is now converted and used by the caravan site as a shop. At the harbour, boats also discharged coal for firing the kilns of the Brick and Tile Works. Grid Ref NJ660659. The harbour is not currently listed.

Blackpots Harbour. (S. Bruce).

1799   The population of Boyndie Parish was 1,260, including 460 in the Seatown of Whitehills.

c1800   The Girnal (Granary) / Warehouse was built at the corner of Low Shore and Seafield Street. This was used for storage of goods for export such as grain and salmon, and for short-term storage of imported goods. Dances were held here in the early part of 20th century. *See 1993.*

Former Girnal, Whitehills.
(S. Bruce).

c1800   The mill was built at Scotsmill. It was formerly used as a pottery. Category B listed. Grid Ref NJ611654.

Scotsmill, millstone sign.
(S. Bruce).

c1800

Milton of Tillynaught Bridge with a huge crack 8th Nov 2009, it collapsed and was completely lost 12th Nov 2009. (S. Bruce)

c1800 The twenty-two foot long single span rubble built bridge over the Burn of Boyne at Milton of Tillynaught was built. The Burn of Boyne forms part of the boundary between Boyndie and Fordyce Parishes. The bridge collapsed in **2009** after being weakened by excessive rainfalls. According to the Banffshire Journal an earlier bridge collapsed here in 1730. Category B listed by Historic Scotland. Grid Ref NJ598610.

1801 The population of Boyndie Parish was 1,122.

1801 The Books of Presbytery of Boyndie Kirk record that forty boys were being taught in the parochial school, and in the parish a woman was teaching a few children the elements of reading and the catechism (The principles of Christianity).

1809 Mill of Boyndie Farmhouse was built fronting an 18th century single storey building which now forms the rear wing. The Mill itself no longer exists. The Mill was owned by the Milne family for at least two centuries. *See 1738*. Grid Ref NJ583638. Category B listed.

1811 The population of Boyndie was 1,128.

1814 The Boyndie Kirk Session gave metal badges with the name of the Parish inscribed on them to three poor parishioners. This was a poor badge, which allowed these persons to beg.

1815 The Seafield Estates, who were the village superiors at the time, built the first harbour at Whitehills just east of the Hythe. Many harbours along the Moray Firth were established around this date due to the herring fishing. This early harbour had two small basins, which allowed boats a bit larger than the fishermen's cobbles to use it. The water depth is said to have been ten to eleven feet at Spring tides. Herring fishermen used the harbour to land their catch, and for its export. Salt was imported for the curing of the herring. In the latter half of the 19th century up to 150 small fishing boats Skaffie's, and later Zulu's used this harbour. Downies fish factory was later built on the site of the filled-in harbour. Downies in Whitehills have been in the fish business for over 120 years. *See 1900*.

1821 The population of Boyndie was 1,290.

The Old Harbour, Whitehills pre-1900. (Courtesy J. Ritchie).

1821   During his journey all around the British coast artist William Daniell (1769 to 1837) R.A. (Royal Academy) drew this painting (In colour) of Boyne Castle. The castle has severely deteriorated since this was painted; see *c1580* for a recent photograph. Grid Ref NJ612657. *See 1836.*

Boyne Castle 1821. (William Daniell R.A.).

1824   Banff Distillery was first established by James Mckilligan & Co., at the 'Mill of Banff', near Colleonard. Approximate grid ref NJ678626. *See 1863, 1877, 1932, 1941, 1983, 1985, and 1991.*

1825   Knock House No's 10 and 10A, Knock Street was built as a farmhouse by A. Murray. Datestone above the door has in fine lettering the initials 'HW' for Henry Watson and the date 1825. Category B listed by Historic Scotland.

Knock House No. 10 & 10A Knock Street. Mr. & Mrs Watson at the door. (S. Bruce).

1829   John Wilson Esq. of Brangan introduced a Teeswater bull to his farm, this was the first of this breed in the Boyndie Parish.

1831   The population of Boyndie Parish was 1,501.

1832   Almost the entire population of Whitehills except two old and infirm men marched to Banff to attend the 'Great Reform Meeting'. The Scottish Reform Act of 1832 was passed by Parliament. This Act changed the Election Law, meaning more MP's were elected, which gave a better representation of the counties of Scotland.

1834   Thomas Edward (*1814* to *1886*) a shoemaker born in Gosport settled in Banff. At the age of twenty-three, he met Sophia Reid (1815 to 1890), a local girl from Boyndie whom he married, and they settled in Banff. Thomas later became famous as a Naturalist. The story of Thomas Edward's life and work is recorded in a book titled 'The Life of A Scotch Naturalist – Thomas Edward – Nature and Natural History', written by Samuel Smiles and first published in 1876. Smiles' Biography brought

Naturalist – Thomas Edward. (Fred Bremner).

Thomas Edward to the attention of Queen Victoria (1819 to 1901) who was so impressed by him and his work that she awarded him a pension of £50 per annum, which was twice as much as he usually earned as a shoemaker.

1834   A new church with seats for 250, and a manse were built at Ord, this was to accommodate Parishioners living in the south of Boyndie Parish, those who felt it was too far to travel to St. Brandon's at Boyndie. Grid Ref

Boyne Castle painting of 1836.

NJ623584. The Ord Parish War Memorial, which commemorates the dead of WW1 and WW2 stands adjacent to the former church, now converted to a house. *See 1869.*

1834   The Boyndie Kirk Session gave a loan of £25 to the managers of the school lately erected in Whitehills.

1836   Boyne Castle was painted, and the ruin was depicted as greatly deteriorated compared to the painting of *1821*. (See above).

1837   In this year, eleven people of Boyndie Parish died of influenza.

1839   30th June – The Edinburgh Caledonian Mercury reported the following: "Melancholy Accident – Three Lives Lost. On Thursday last, the 30th ultimo, a coble, belonging to the salmon fishing station of Messrs Hogarth, adjacent to Whitehills, left the harbour at Blackpots, about eleven o'clock forenoon, for the purpose of bringing on shore their bag-net, which, owing to the violence of the surf, was apparently driving among the rocks, where it would have been soon torn to pieces. The coble was manned by four men, Charles Maclean, James Robertson, and two lads from Rosemarkie, near Cromarty, who, proceeding towards the net, the boat swung round broadside on to the wave, and was struck by a heavy sea, and three of the men precipitated into the water. One of them regained the boat, which had (relieved of the men) again righted, but was full of water. This young man being an excellent swimmer, rashly resolved, by the assistance of the boat, to clear himself of the incumbrance of his clothes, and swim on shore, which, having partly effected, the boat being then sunk to the gunwales, he left her to make the attempt; but the tide then running strong, and the surf very violent, he was soon exhausted, and with much difficulty reached the rocks, where he was dashed by a tremendous wave upon the very first rock he reached, and killed on the spot; his body has not yet been recovered. The two others, for a very brief space, were seen struggling violently in the surf, but soon disappeared. One of them kept hold of the boat, and drifted with her on shore, but so exhausted that up to this day (Monday) his recovery is doubtful. The two bodies recovered were decently interred in the Churchyard of Boyndie. Charles Maclean and James Robertson have left widows and families, in poor circumstances, to deplore their sudden and untimely fate. In the end we deem it fair to state, that the fishermen of Whitehills, on learning the catastrophe, hastened to the spot, boldly facing the raging surf, to afford assistance, so far as practicable; but we are sorry to say the fate of the unfortunate sufferers was sealed before their arrival."

1840 The Methodist Chapel No. 4 Chapel Street, Whitehills was built. It is one of the earliest surviving Methodist Chapels in the north east of Scotland. It is now used as the Watergaw Ceramics Studio Pottery. Category B listed.

Watergaw Ceramics, Studio Pottery, in the former Methodist Chapel building, No. 4 Chapel Street. (S. Bruce).

1841 The population of Boyndie Parish was 1,501, with 523 living in Whitehills.

1841-2

St. Brandon's House.
(S.Bruce).

Watergaw Ceramics Studio Pottery sign, No. 4 Chapel Street. (S. Bruce).

1841-2 The Church of Scotland Manse and U plan steading at Boyndie was built to the design of architect William Robertson of Elgin, replacing an earlier Manse built *c1775*, which stood fifty yards to the rear. The manse is currently privately owned and now known as St. Brandon's House. Category B listed. Grid Ref NJ643639.

1842 The Church of Scotland Minister of the Boyndie Parish recorded that he and his Whitehills congregation were 'liberally allowed' the use of the Methodist Chapel on 'Sabbath evenings'.

1842 An infant school was established in Whitehills supported by voluntary contributions from the Honourable Mrs. Grant and others.

1842 A Late Bronze Age (*1,000 to 700BC*) sword was found at the Boar's Moss, Blairshinnoch, Boyndie. In *1945,* it was donated to Elgin Museum. Grid Ref NJ6462.

1843 18th May – Rev. Alexander Anderson the Minister of St. Brandon's Church attended the General Assembly. An incident commonly referred to as the 'Disruption', led to the Minister and all twelve Elders of St. Brandon's Church breaking away and instituting a 'Free Church in Boindie'. With no church, services were held in Cairnton Schoolhouse, Boyndie. The congregation were allowed use of the Methodist Weslyan Chapel, Chapel Street, Whitehills on Sabbath evenings.

1844   The United Free Church erected a new church capable of seating 250 and a manse in Reidhaven Street, Whitehills. This church was used until *1925/6.*

18th May 1843 Boindie Free Church Communion Token. (Courtesy Isobel Watt).

1845   At St. Brandon's Stones an urn containing defaced coins were found underneath one of the stones. *See c2000BC , and 1003.*

1851   The population of Boyndie was 1,564.

1857   An Act for the 'Care and Treatment of Lunatics and for the Provision and Maintenance and Regulation of Lunatic Asylums in Scotland' was passed by Parliament. This led to the building of Banff District Asylum (Ladysbridge Hospital) in *1863-5.*

1857   27th July – Banff to Tillynaught Railway was authorised by the Government. *See 1859, 1863, 1867, 1964, and 1968.*

Tillynaught Railway Bridge. (S. Bruce).

1858   The Whitehills Barometer was located near the Old Harbour on the gable end of No. 37 Low Shore. It was provided by the Board of Trade for the fishermen of Whitehills. Vice-Admiral Robert Fitzroy (1805 to 1865) former Naval Hydrographer born in Suffolk believed that many ships and lives were lost at sea because the fishermen left port unaware of coming storms. In order to remedy this he had a specially designed 'Fishery Barometer' issued to every port. Their large clear scales bear 'Fitzroy's Rules'. The ports that could not afford one got theirs free from the Board of Trade, others had to pay or have it paid for by local businesses. Fitzroy's Barometers must have saved thousands of lives over the years. The Whitehills Barometer was made by Negretti and Zambra's of London, and bears serial number F.B. No. 12. It was removed from the original box on Low Shore, and re-sited at the Harbour Masters Office, where it can be seen today.

1858 Barometer Housing, No. 37 Low Shore, Whitehills. (S. Bruce).

1859   2nd August – The Banff to Tillynaught Railway service via Ladysbridge fully opened. A single train first ran on the 30th July, but was derailed. A four arch bridge over the Boyndie Burn was built. The bridge does not appear to be listed. Grid Ref NJ667643. *See 1857, 1863, 1867, 1964, and 1968.*

Railway Bridge c1859 at Banff Distillery, Inverboyndie. (S. Bruce).

1860   An RNLI framed certificate dated 10th December 1959 in Whitehills Parish Church, Seafield Street commemorates the first lifeboat station established in Whitehills in 1860. *See 1922, 1932, 1959, 1961, 1969, and 2008.*

c1860   Boyndie Parish School was built. It was formally gifted to the

School Board of Boyndie Parish by Rt. Hon. Sir John Charles Ogilvie-Grant (1815 to 1881) 7th Earl of Seafield on the 17th January 1878.

1861 The population of Boyndie Parish was 1,711.

1863 James Simpson junior who took over Banff Distillery near Colleonard in 1852, built a new distillery at Inverboyndie. Due to the arrival of the railway in *1859,* the site was considered perfect; because it was adjacent to the railway track and to the Burn of Boyndie, which was a much better source of water than the original distillery built by James McKilligan & Co., at the 'Mill of Banff', near Colleonard in *1824.* James Simpson senior and James Simpson junior purchased the Mill of Banff Distillery in 1852. Grid Ref NJ667644.

1863 21st July – The Great North East of Scotland Railway Company (GNoSR) took over the running of the Banff to Tillynaught railway line; it was renamed the Banffshire Railway. It was amalgamated with GNoSR 12th August *1867. See 1857, 1859, 1964, and 1968.*

1864 25th October – Nine Portessie fishermen were lost when the 'Shamrock' BF743 sank off Whitehills.

1865

Former Ladysbridge Hospital and Railway Station c1900.

1865 1st May – Banff County Lunatic Asylum was officially opened. It was built of Rhynie freestone at Ladysbridge to a design by

Architects A. & W. Reid of Inverness. It stood in a prominent, yet secluded setting; and was designed to cater for ninety inmates. The 1857 Lunacy (Scotland) Act required that all Asylums with over one hundred patients had to appoint a residential medical superintendent, so ninety patients kept the Asylum below this requirement.

A separate villa for male patients was built in *1903*, and was extended in the *1950's*. The hospital closed in *2003*. The site is currently no longer used as a hospital and work has commenced for conversion to housing. The Troup, Administration, and Moor Newton range of buildings are category B listed by Historic Scotland. Grid Ref NJ650638.

1866   5th November – George Milne was born in Aberdeen. There is a stone in Inverboyndie Kirk to his memory. The stone reads "Field Marshall Lord Milne 1866 – 1948 he was also descended from the Milne's of the north". He was promoted to Field Marshal in 1928. He was created 1st Baron Milne in

Field Marshal Lord Milne memorial stone, Inverboyndie Kirk. (S. Bruce).

1933. He died 23rd March 1948. His awards were Knight Grand Cross of the Order of the Bath (G.C.B.), Knight Grand Cross of the Order of St. Michael and St. George (G.C.M.G.), and the Distinguished Service Order (D.S.O.).

1866   The house at No. 25 Low Shore, Whitehills was built for Henry Watson. It has a lintel dated 1866 with his initials 'HW'. Category B listed by Historic Scotland. No. 24 Boyne Street has a similar stone, so has its neighbour across the street.

1866 date stone No. 25 Low Shore Whitehills. (A. Bruce).

Date stone No.24 Boyne Street. (S. Bruce).

1859 date stone No. 23 Boyne Street. (A. Bruce).

1867   12th August – The Banffshire Railway established in *1863* was amalgamated with GNoSR. *See 1857, 1859, 1863, 1964 and 1968.*

1869   5th July – Ord was erected a Parish in its own right. *See 1834.*

c1870   No's 8 to 9 Chapel Street, Whitehills was built. This was used as a cartwrights shop, and later as a joiners shop before being converted to a house.

1876   Whitehills School was built in Loch Street. It was designed by architect James Mathews (1819 to 1898) of Aberdeen. It was demolished in *1977*.

Cartwrights, No's. 8 to 9 Chapel Street, Whitehills. (Courtesy Alasdair Walker).

1877   9th May – The main building of Banff Distillery at Inverboyndie was destroyed by fire, however, the maltings and the warehouse were untouched. It was quickly reconstructed and from this date the distillery kept its own fire engine. *See 1824, 1863, 1877, 1932, 1941, 1983, 1985, and 1991.*

1879   The United Free Presbyterian Church was built in Seafield Street, Banff, to the design of Architect Alexander Ross of Inverness.   In *1925-6* it was dismantled and rebuilt and extended by fifteen feet in Seafield Street, Whitehills. Category B listed.

Church down-pipe. (S. Bruce).

The United Presbyterian Church (With no clock), and the former YMCA building Seafield Street, Banff.

1880   1st June – Woodpark Succursal Asylum was opened.   It was built to accommodate "Forty incurable but inoffensive and easily managed females". This was built separate from Ladysbridge Hospital however; it amalgamated with Ladysbridge 29th June 1889. On the 1902 map this is referred to as a Smallpox Hospital.   Approximate Grid Ref NJ656642.

Woodpark Succursal Asylum. (From Ladysbridge Hospital book).

1880 -82   A vestry was added to St. Brandon's Church, Boyndie. Grid
Ref NJ642638. Category B Listed.

1885   9th February – Forbes Scott Tocher
(d.1973) was born in Whitehills.
He graduated Master of Arts
(M.A.) from Aberdeen University
in 1906, and Batchelor of Divinity
(B.D.) from Edinburgh University
in 1909. In 1909, he was ordained
in St. Brandon's Parish Church,
Boyndie. From 1909 to 1915, he
worked in Ichang, China as a
missionary.   He   returned   to
Scotland to serve in WW1 in the
Royal Field Artillery, first as a
gunner, then as a Commissioned
officer, where he was awarded a
Military Cross (M.C.) for bravery.
He returned to China after WW1

Forbes Scott Tocher.
(Courtesy Botriphnie
Church).

To continue his missionary work and in 1928, he was made
Commander of the British Empire (C.B.E.) after he participated
in the rescue of Captain Lalor of the steamship 'Soiangtan' who
had been kidnapped from his ship by pirates. In recognition of
his missionary work, he was in 1934 made an honorary Doctor
of Divinity by Aberdeen University. He returned to Scotland in
1948, but only after being taken prisoner by the Japanese in
1940, and held in Shanghai until 1945. From 1948 to 1958, he
served as Minister at Botriphnie Church.   He spent his
retirement in Banff where he died 15th August 1973.

1886   William Cramond A.M., (Schoolmaster of Cullen) wrote a book
titled 'The Church and Churchyard of Boyndie'. It was printed
by the Banffshire Journal.

1890   W. Anderson and P. Burnett excavated a mound near the mouth
of the Burn of Boyndie, now a grass covered sand dune. Inside
the mound they found shells, bones, pieces of charcoal,
burned and glazed pottery, and they concluded that this was

possibly a Midden used in pre-historic times by early settlers. Grid Ref NJ66686484.

1890   The County of Banff (Banffshire) was established. On the Moray Firth Coast, it stretched from a little west of Portgordon in the west to Cullykhan in the east. The southernmost tip was fifty-nine miles south of the Moray Firth in the Cairngorms. The highest peak in the shire being Ben Macdhui at 4,296 feet high. The Parish of St. Fergus near Peterhead was also part of Banffshire, due to a link with the Cheyne family. In *1975*

Banffshire coat-of-arms.

The County was broken-up, simply put: it was split between Aberdeenshire and Moray.

1890   20th January – A public meeting was held in Whitehills to discuss the need for a new harbour. See *1895* and *1900*.

1891   The population of Boyndie Parish was 2,113, with 602 living in Whitehills. Most common names were Lovy (Lovie), Watson, and Ritchie.

1892   William Henry (Reay) Buchanan Mirrlees was born. There is a stone in Inverboyndie Kirk to his memory. The stone reads "Major-General Reay Mirrlees 1892 to 1964 stepfather and foster father of Robin De La Lanne-Mirrlees formerly Grinnell-Milne". He was promoted to Major-General in the Royal Field Artillery. He retired from the army in 1946. His awards are as follows: Order of the Bath (C.B.), Distinguished Service Order (D.S.O.) and the Military Cross (M.C.). William known as Reay went to the orphanage school in Aberlour. He died 22nd October 1964.

1895   The first Commissioners (Trustees) of Whitehills Harbour were elected by an Act of Parliament known as 'Whitehills Pier and Harbour Orders Act'. *See 1900*.

1895   20th July to 3rd September – James Clarke Hook (1819 to 1907)

R.A. born in London visited Whitehills and lodged with Mrs Henry Watson No. 6 New Street. During his visit, he is known to have painted three paintings 1) Breadwinners of the North (Boat), 2) Roadside, and 3) Little Farm. These are all in private collections, however some of his work is in the collection of the Aberdeen Art Gallery.

1900   Whitehills Harbour was built in the form we see it today. This harbour replaced two small, usually cramped basins, which stood where Downie's fish factory currently stands. From this date forward, the Harbour has been run and maintained by nine elected Commissioners. See *1959*.

Late   At Boyndie Parish Church (Church of Scotland), a Beadle's
19th C Cottage and Steading were built. These two buildings have since been joined with an extension and are now holiday homes. Category B listed. Grid Ref NJ642639.

Former Beadles Cottages, St. Brandon's, Boyndie. (A. Bruce).

c1900

Whitehills from the west c1900 (Courtesy Isobel Watt).

1901   A Mission Hall later known as St. Brandon's Church Centre in Seafield Street was built. The Rev. Jimmie G. Ledingham, Minister of Boyndie Church from 1895 to 1941, part-funded its build, other funds were raised by the Ladies of the Work Party who held bazaars. His initials 'JGL' and the date 1901 adorn the buildings porch. His father James Ledingham preceded him as the Minister from 1863 to 1895. This hall was used before the union of the church with Trinity Church, as a place for evening worship by the St. Brandon's congregation, and as a meeting place for Church organisations. *See 2005.*

St. Brandon's Church Centre, Seafield Street. (S. Bruce).

The Hythe, Whitehills, c1900. (BM&HA Archive).

1901

JGL / 1901 date stone, St. Brandon's Church Hall, Seafield Street, Whitehills. (S. Bruce).

Left – Rev. J. Ledingham senior and his sister Elsie. (Photo courtesy of Isobel Watt).

1901   The population of Boyndie was 2,005.

1902   Nether Dallachy farmhouse was built. A date stone above the front door bears this date.

Nether Dallachy Farm 1902 date stone. (A. Bruce).

1904   15th December – The 145.8 feet long x 281 GRT Glasgow steamship 'Nar' carrying a cargo of coal from Sunderland to Burghead foundered off Spey Mouth during a storm. Her crew of nine were all lost. The ships bell can be seen in the window of the Whitehills Harbour Master's office.

1910   St. Brandon's Church at Boyndie was extensively altered internally. This included removal of two galleries and extension to the other. Pews were rearranged to face the new pitch pine pulpit. A new large coloured glass window was inserted into the gable wall providing much needed light along the length of the building. A pipe organ was added, half of the cost was funded by Sir Andrew Carnegie, the other half by the fund-raising efforts of the Ladies Work Party.

1910   Whitehills Public Hall, Reidhaven Street was built as a 'Public Hall, Library and Reading Room' and from the day it opened, it was the hub of the community. It was used for all sorts of community events, including sales, weddings, dances, plays and concerts, etc. The building cost of the hall was funded by Dunfermline born Andrew Carnegie (1835 to 1919) who had made his fortune in America. Prior to Carnegie's generous donation the town had plans for erecting a hall. These however had to be amended to suit Carnegie who insisted the hall included a library and reading room. A library and reading room were included in the plans and two large cupboards placed in the hall for books, but no books were ever provided; and the unused cupboards were eventually moved to the school, where they were used for storage purposes. The hall was upgraded some years ago following a major fundraising effort and the building is still widely used by local groups.

Whitehills Public Hall, Reidhaven Street. (S. Bruce).

Andrew Carnegie. (Columbia Library).

1910 date stone. (S. Bruce).

c1910

Gutting Quines at Whitehills. (Courtesy Annie Milne).

c1910

Whitehills fishermen, mending their nets.
(Courtesy of Whitehills and District Community Council).

c1910

Gutting quines and coopers, Downie's, Whitehills.
(Courtesy of Whitehills and District Community Council).

c1910

Steam Drifters in Whitehills Harbour c1910.
(Courtesy of Whitehills and District Community Council).

c1900   At the end of the 19th century the village still had many local trades, such as bakers, butchers, cartwrights etc. An interesting carving of a boot left by a shoemaker can be seen at No. 5 Reidhaven Street.

Former windowpane from the door of the shoemakers shop No. 5 Reidhaven Street.

Shoemakers House, No. 5 Reidhaven Street. (S. Bruce).
Shoe maker's window reproduced by permission of Aberdeenshire Museums Service and © Aberdeenshire Council.

1911   The population of Boyndie was 2,178.

1915   The Police Station No. 6 Reidhaven Street was built. It has since been converted to a house.

1916   20th February – Banff registered drifter BF92 'Gavenwood' was sunk by a mine ten nautical miles east of Brindisi, Italy. She was built in Banff in 1914 by W. & G. Stephen for Macduff owners. In 1915, she was requisitioned by the Admiralty for use as a net barrier tender. Nine crew and two officers were all lost including Petty Officer Francis Hendry a native of Whitehills. His name is on the Parish War Memorial. (Admiralty drifter no. 2104)

WW1   Corporal James Mitchell of the Machine Gun Corps (Infantry) 152nd Company was awarded a Military Medal (M.M.) for bravery. He died in service 29th May 1917. Service number 73465. His name is on the Arras Memorial, France. *See Appendix F.*

WW1   Private Henry G. Legge of the 1st Battalion the Gordon Highlander's was awarded a Military Medal (M.M.) for bravery. He died in service 23rd October 1918. Service number 240551. His name is on the Romerie Communal Cemetery

WW1 Extension Memorial, France.
*See **Appendix F**.*

c1920 The Boyndie Parish War Memorial was erected in Seafield Street, Whitehills. It was designed by architect Malcolm Sinclair McCallum (c1887 to 1928) of Cullen. The War Memorial commemorates the dead of WW1 and WW2. Inside Whitehills Parish Church is a beautifully presented book with the Rolls of Honour for WW1 and WW2. This book was commissioned by Kirk Session to compensate for the loss of memorial tablets following a fire at St. Brandon's Church, Boyndie. See ***Appendix F*** and ***Appendix G*** for WW1 and WW2 Rolls of Honour.

WW1 Military Medal.

Soldier. (S. Bruce).

Sailor. (S. Bruce).

1921 Due to the collapse of the herring market, herring fishing virtually ceased. Whitehills fishermen opted to use the Seine net, or to go trawling.

1921 The population of Boyndie was 2,118.

1922   After successful fund-raising by the Ladies Work Party a new porch was added to the west gable of St. Brandon's, Boyndie Parish Church (Built in *1773*).

1922 date stone St. Brandon's, Boyndie Parish Church. (S. Bruce).

1924   January – The main lifeboat station for the area was transferred from Banff Bridge to Whitehills. The reasoning behind this was that Macduff fishermen were fishing further away from port than the Whitehills men so Whitehills was better placed to man the boat. A new lifeboat RNLB 'George and Mary Berrey' was stationed at Whitehills. It was 35 feet long, 8.5 feet beam and self-righting. Official number 479. This boat was launched eight times and saved seven lives, and served until *1928*. The station remained at Whitehills until *1969*, when it was transferred to Macduff. *See 1860, 1932, 1948, 1969, and 2005.*

The Auld Boat', Low Shore, Whitehills. Names left to right: George Findlay (Shirvie), Raffan (Ponzon), Joseph Watson, Willie Joiner, Alex Watson, Henry Ritchie (Ditz), Jimmy Inglis, William Joiner, George Findlay, Alex Lawrence, and Alex Findlay. (Courtesy of George Lovie).

1925   The photo above of an upturned boat known as the 'Auld Boat' was taken at the Low Shore, Whitehills. The 'Auld Boat' (shed) was a feature of Whitehills waterfront until the great gale of 1953. Fishermen stored their nets here, and they mended nets outside it. The men shown are thought to have gathered for a good gossip. Many of the old sailing drifters were drawn up on the beach, but most of them were broken up for firewood.

1925/6

Whitehills Parish Church, Seafield Street. (S. Bruce).

1925/6   The United Free Presbyterian Church, which had stood in Seafield Street, Banff since **1879**, was taken down stone by stone, and rebuilt in Seafield Street, Whitehills, (extended to be 15 feet longer), where it became the Boyndie Trinity U.F. Church (Now the Whitehills Parish Church). The original architect was Alexander Ross of Inverness. This church replaced the church in Reidhaven Street, which was too small and needing costly repairs. The foundation stone of the church was officially laid by Nina Caroline Studley-Herbert (1906 to 1969) 12th Countess of Seafield in the summer of 1926, and local tradesmen quickly rebuilt the church with it opening later in 1926. As part of the re-building the tower was heightened and a four-face clock was donated by the Misses Adamson, in memory of their parents. Dr. A. Barclay

Lyon and Dr. George Lyon gifted a communion table and chair both of carved oak, in memory of their parents and grandparents. Mr. Henry Napier gifted an inside clock in memory of his sister and brother-in-law, John and Jeannie Brown. The village town crier's bell of *1727* is encased and displayed in the church. *See 1968.*

1928   A new lifeboat RNLB 'George Gordon Moir' was stationed at Whitehills. It was 35 feet long, 10 feet beam and self-righting. Official number 606. This boat was launched only once, saved no lives, and served until *1932.*

1929   Peter Anson (1889 to 1975) artist and writer visited the Moray Firth and drew many drawings and water-colour paintings of harbours and fishing boats, including this drawing of Whitehills Harbour. The wooden building in the bottom-right of the drawing was George Ritchie's Fish House, which has since been demolished.

Whitehills Harbour as drawn by Peter Anson in 1929.

1931   Whitehills Harbour was deepened. Six feet was cleared from the bottom of the channel and the outside dock.

1931   The population of Boyndie was 2,014.

1932   A new lifeboat was stationed at Whitehills by the RNLI it was the 'RNLB Civil Service No. 4', it was a 35.5 feet long self-righting boat, official number 756. It was launched 26 times, saved nine lives, and served until *1948*. The boat was built by J. Samuel White of Cowes, Isle of Wight, and cost £3,342. It was powered by a Weyburn AE6 petrol engine, which produced 35 BHP. *See 1860, 1933, and 2005.*

1932   March – SMD bought Banff Distillery at Inverboyndie.

1933   Boyne Castle built *c1580* was listed as an Ancient Scheduled Monument. It is likely the sign shown was erected because of this newly acquired classification. Grid Ref NJ611656.

Sign on Boyne Castle wall. (S. Bruce).

The sign reads – "ANCIENT MONUMENTS ACTS 1913 AND 1931. ANY PERSON WHO INJURES OR DEFACES THIS MONUMENT MAY BE FINED AND ORDERED TO PAY THE COSTS OF REPAIRS OR BE IMPRISONED".

1933   The RNLI Lifeboat Shed was built at Whitehills Harbour. *See 1860, 1932, and 2005.*

1930's

Seafield Street, Whitehills (1930's).

1936   4th December – A member of the crew of the Whitehills Lifeboat 'RNLB Civil Service No. 4' was washed overboard; he was saved and made a full recovery.

c1940 The Whitehills Parish Church Outreach and Mission New Haul, in Loch Street was originally built as a temporary garage to house the fire engine during WW2. The Church of God bought the hall for £10 from the council in 1948, and it was used as a hall until 2000. It was for many years known as the Brethren Hall. It was until 2010 used as a charity shop.

Former Whitehills Parish Church, Outreach and Mission New Haul, Loch Street. (S. Bruce).

1941   Boyndie New Cemetery was established. Grid Ref NJ664646.

1941   16th August – Banff Distillery at Inverboyndie was bombed by a German Junkers Ju-88 bomber plane. No. 12 warehouse took a direct hit and it is said that due to the bombing so much whisky was flowing down the Burn of Boyndie that several cows and birds became intoxicated. Grid Ref NJ667643.

1942-3 RAF Banff Coastal Command at Boyndie Aerodrome four miles west of Banff was built using truckloads of sand from the beach at Banff. This removed the bar at the mouth of the Deveron. The site rivalled Lossiemouth and Kinloss in terms of scale, and had a 6,000 feet long runway running west to east. During WW2 eight squadrons were stationed here as follows:

143 – British, 144 – British, 235 – British, 248 – British, 333 – Norwegian, 404 – Canadian, 445 – Australian, and 489 – New Zealand; the crews flew Bristol Beaufighter and Mosquito planes.

1942-5 The airmen played a major part during WW2 by attacking the German shipping fleets and submarines along the west coast of Norway, thereby denying the Germans vital supplies.

Beaufighter 404 Squadron.

However, it was a dangerous job and 81 RAF Banff Strike Wing aircrew died on operations. In Banff Parish Church is a plaque and a Book of Remembrance, which contains the 81 names of the airmen who died

Mosquito.

during WW2. Some are buried in a section of Banff Cemetery. Coastal Command also had a satellite at Dallachy approximately 20 miles further west. Grid Ref's: RAF Banff NJ6164, & RAF Dallachy NJ3663.

248 Squadron. (Photos courtesy John Duncan of Sketraw).

1942   Boyndie Airfield, Operations Block was built by Wimpey Construction. Inside the building are the remains of hand-painted information on lost aircraft and crews, and vessels sunk by the airmen. Canadian war artist Don Anderson is reputed as having started the wall charts. A replica of the tally board can be seen in the RAF Banff display inside the

Boyndie Visitors Centre. Category B listed.

1943   Boyndie Airfield Control Tower was built. It was renovated in *1976*. Category B listed.

1943   5th April – RAF Banff was transferred to the control of 21 Group Flying Training Command.

1943   21st April – RAF Banff Airfield was officially opened. The first year of operation consisted mainly of pilot training by Unit 14 (Pilot) Advanced Flying Unit (AFU) using twin-engined Airspeed Oxford planes. 1,516 pilots were trained here in a period of twelve months. Unit 14 remained at the aerodrome until August 1944 and trained 2,136 pilots during their 15 months at Boyndie.

1944   September – The training aircraft at RAF Banff were replaced with Mk10 Bristol Beaufighters and FB VI Mosquitoes.

1944   1st September – RAF Banff was taken over by 18 Group Coastal Command. The commanding officer was Group Captain Max Aitken (1910 to 1985) D.S.O., D.F.C., son of Max Aitken (1879 to 1964) 1st Baron Beaverbrook. The Coastal Command comprised of six multi-national squadrons 143 – British, 144 – British, 235 – British, 248 – British, 333 – Norwegian, and 404 – Canadian. *See 1976.*

1944   26th December – A detachment of 279 Squadron Warwick planes from RAF Banff were based at RAF Fraserburgh. This deployment was for air / sea rescue duties, for the Strike Wings at RAF Banff and RAF Dallachy.

c1945   A new fish market and harbour office was built. *See 1954.*

1945   March – Squadron 404 moved from Dallachy to RAF Banff.

1945   25th May – The last Mosquito plane flew from RAF Banff. Mosquito's continue to fly after 'Victory in Europe Day' (VE Day) due to the fear of attack from German submarines who had not surrendered. At this time there were 3,000 personnel stationed at RAF Banff.

1945   Mrs Gordon Duff donated a late Bronze Age sword (*1000 to 700BC*) to Elgin Museum. It was found in *1842* at the Boar's Moss, Boyndie. Grid Ref NJ6462.

1946   Summer – RAF Banff Boyndie Aerodrome closed, during its peak phase of operation it had a complement of around 3,000 including several hundred WAAF. The Aerodrome was later used by the Royal Navy as a target for simulated bombing attacks by aircraft from RAF Lossiemouth. *See 1989.*

1946   27th December – Herbert John Green born in Boyndie died aged forty. *See Appendix I.*

1948   The congregations of St. Brandon's, Boyndie, and the Boyndie Trinity U.F. Church, Seafield Street were united. Morning services were held at St. Brandon's and evening services in Whitehills.

1948   8th April – Whitehills Lifeboat 'RNLB Civil Service No. 4' was wrecked on rocks; no lives were lost.

1948   A new lifeboat – RNLB 'William Maynard' was stationed at Whitehills. It was 40 feet long, 10.5 feet beam and self-righting." Official number 746. This boat was launched three times, saved no lives, and served until *1949. See 1860, 1932, 1933, 1961, 1969, and 2005.*

1949   The Trinity Church, Seafield Street, Whitehills and St. Brandons' Kirk, Boyndie were united. *See 1996.*

1949   A new lifeboat – RNLB 'Thomas Markby' was stationed at Whitehills. It was 40 feet long, 10.5 feet beam and self-righting." Official number 706. This boat was launched five times, saved no lives, and served until *1952. See 1860, 1932, 1933,* 1948, *1961, 1969, and 2005.*

1952   A new lifeboat – RNLB 'St. Andrew (Civil Service No. 10)' was stationed at Whitehills. It was 41 feet long, 11.75 feet beam and self-righting." Official number 897. This boat was launched nine times, saved no lives, and served until *1960. See 1860, 1932, 1933,* 1948, 1949, *1961, 1969, and 2005.*

1953   Every child in Banffshire was invited to a party in No. 1 Hangar, Boyndie Aerodrome to celebrate the coronation of Queen Elizabeth II (b.1926). After WW2, during the period of rationing the hangers at Boyndie Aerodrome were used as an egg store and distribution centre for the supply of eggs to the whole of Scotland.

1953   31st January to 1st February – A great storm hit the Moray Firth coastline, and Whitehills like other fishing communities was badly affected. Many houses were flooded and virtually all of the 'Sheddies' on the shore were destroyed.

1954   A covered fish market was built at Whitehills.

1955   A sea wall was built along Low Shore, Whitehills.

1959   10th December – A letter (Memento) to one hundred years of lifeboat service was written by the RNLI. It is on display in Whitehills Parish Church, Seafield Street. *See 1860.*

1959   October – Coppersmiths while doing work on a still at Banff Distillery, Inverboyndie caused an explosion and a fire, which closed the distillery for several weeks.

1959   18th November – The Whitehills Lifeboat 'RNLB St. Andrew' was broached-to on service, and one crewmember was washed overboard. He was saved and made a full recovery.

1959-61   Due to an increasing fishing fleet Whitehills Harbour was extensively deepened (By approx six feet). During these works, which cost £100,000 the Whitehills fleet berthed in Macduff. During the construction work, thirty tons of stones and mortar from one of the quays collapsed.

A packed Macduff Harbour including the Whitehills fleet c1960. (BM&HA).

1960   A new lifeboat – RNLB 'Sarah Wood and William David Crossweller' was stationed at Whitehills. It was 45.5 feet long, 12.5 feet beam and self-righting. Official number 716. This boat was launched once, saved no lives, and served until *1961*. See *1860, 1932, 1933, 1948, 1949, 1961, 1969, and 2005*.

1961   14th August – HRH Queen Elizabeth II (b.1926) and the Duke of Edinburgh (b.1921) made a visit to Whitehills on their tour of the Moray Firth. They originally did not plan to stop at Whitehills but thanks to the efforts of Rev. Alexander W. Grieg, Whitehills was included in the Royal Tour.

1961   August – The RNLI launched a new 47 feet long Watson class lifeboat at Whitehills. The new lifeboat was officially launched and named by Caroline Dewar (b.1934) Duchess of Fife and was called the 'Helen Wycherley.' The new lifeboat was built for the RNLI in 1961 by Groves & Guttridge at Cowes on the Isle of Wight. It was 47 feet long, 13 feet beam and had a draft of 4 ½ feet. Official number 959. She was launched eleven times, saved one life, and served at Whitehills from June 1961 until *1969*. This boat was converted to an angling charter boat and was recorded as seen in Whitby in 2008.

'RNLB Helen Wycherley'.

1962 Grampian Go-cart Club, Boyndie was founded. One of the founder members was Lord Seafield who made it all possible by providing the Boyndie Aerodrome for the use of the club.

A go-carter in action at Boyndie Aerodrome. (S. Bruce).

1963 Whitehills Primary School was granted the use of their own coat of arms.

1964 6th July – The Tillynaught to Banff railway line was closed to passengers, however it remained open to freight. *See 1857, 1859, 1863, 1867, and 1968.*

1967 1st December – The Banffshire Journal published 'Thomas Ruddiman M.A. 1674 – 1757, Keeper, Advocates' Library' by Alexander Allan Cormack.

1968 16th October - James Brown was lost at sea off Kinnaird Head. He was a crewmember of the 'Diligence'. A stained glass window made at Pluscarden Abbey was installed in the Parish Church, Seafield Street in *1970* to his memory.

Stained glass window in memory of James Brown. Whitehills Parish Church. (S. Bruce).

1968 6th May – The Tillynaught to Banff railway line was closed completely. Part of the old line is now used as a walk. *See 1857, 1859, 1863, 1867, 1964, and c1970.*

1969 A sculpture depicting four figures sculpted by 32-year-old Alistair Smart of the Duncan of Jordanstone College of Art in Dundee was erected in the grounds of Ladysbridge Hospital. It was described as being "Of undoubted artistic merit".

1969   July – The Whitehills RNLI station, which opened in **1922,** was closed. The Whitehills lifeboat 'RNLB Helen Wycherley' was transferred to Courtmacsherry, Ireland. Macduff became the main lifeboat station for this stretch of the coast. *See **1860, 1932, 1948, 1959, 1961,** and **2005.***

1969   The Hydro Electric Company proposed the building of a nuclear power station at Stake Ness, west of Whitehills. This £85 million pound project never materialised. Today we have the much safer Boyndie Windfarm providing renewable energy.

c1970   A new playing field was established at Blackpots. The old railway station building from Ladysbridge was set up as a pavilion. Grid Ref NJ658658. *See **1968.***

Whitehills Playing Field Pavilion, Blackpots 2005. (S. Bruce).

c1970   The Post Office opened at No. 23 Seafield Street, Whitehills. It was formerly sited in Reidhaven Street.

Whitehills Post Office. (S. Bruce).

c1972   Whitehills Community Council was established. This was the first Community Council established in Banff and Buchan.

1972   Most of the fisher cottages and house in the Seatown were included in a new conservation area. Many were category C(S) listed by Historic Scotland on the 22nd February 1972.

1973   The Blackpots Brick and Tile Works established *c1788* was sold by the Brodie family who had owned it since 1900, to Mr. John Steele of Kirkhill Farm, who sold it in 1977.

1974   A fishing boat was erected in the Blackpots Playing Field for the children to play in; it was named the 'Bairns Pride' and given registration WS74, WS for Whitehills and 74 for the date.

1974   The Blackpots Brick and Tile Works closed down. *See c1788.*

1976   2nd June - The Boyndie Aerodrome Control Tower was renovated and Banff Amateur Flying Club was officially opened by Group Captain Max Aitken (1910 to 1985) 2nd Baron Beaverbrook, D.S.O., D.F.C., who was the Commander of Boyndie Aerodrome during WW2. To mark the occasion a Mosquito B35 plane landed on the runway alongside the members planes. The club closed in the mid 1980's. *See 1944.*

1977   The 'Old School' in Loch Street built in *1876* was demolished, and a new primary school built in Forbes Road. The bell tower from the old school was re-used as a garden feature in the 'Old School Court' housing development.

1977   The Blackpots Brick and Tile Works established *c1788* was sold and then demolished. A residential caravan site was built on the site. The old Salmon Bothy was converted to the caravan site shop and office. In the 1980's the caravan site was extended further back up the hill (Claybrae). *See 1974.*

Old School bell tower, Old School Court, Whitehills.
(S. Bruce).

Playpark, caravan site and former salmon bothy, Blackpots, Whitehills. (S. Bruce).

1983   May – Banff Distillery at Inverboyndie was closed. The majority of the buildings were demolished in **1985**. However, several of the warehouses although in a dilapidated condition still stand today. Grid Ref NJ667644. *See* **1824, 1863, 1877, 1932, 1941,** *and* **1991.**

Banff Distillery, Inverboyndie, 2007. (S. Bruce).

1985   The main distillery buildings at Banff Distillery, Inverboyndie were demolished. *See* **1824, 1863, 1877, 1932, 1941, 1983,** *and* **1991.**

No 12 Duty Free Warehouse, Banff Distillery, Inverboyndie. (S. Bruce).

1989 28th September – RAF Banff Strike Wing Memorial Trust unveiled a granite memorial in the lay-by on the A98 between Banff and Portsoy near to where the aerodrome was located. It was officially unveiled by Group Captain Bill Sise, former Commanding Officer 248 Squadron, RAF Banff.

Part of the celebrations included a fly past of the last surviving Mosquito, two Buccaneers, and a Nimrod. The six Coastal Command squadrons each have a tree planted in the lay-by to their memory. Grid Ref NJ617624. *See 1943-4, and 2007.*

RAF Banff Memorial.
(S. Bruce).

Banff Strike Wing Memorial. (S. Bruce).

1990   1st January – Sixteen-year old schoolboy Christopher Christie of Whitehills had a ghostly experience on the Red Well Road. He reported that he met an old woman less than five feet tall with a pale face and sagging cheeks, dressed in black who walked straight through his body. As he fled, the woman appeared in front of him repeatedly and each time walked straight through his body. Later while asleep Christopher reported that he awoke struggling for breath and saw a black cloud drift towards his window and vanish. It seems the ghost followed him home. In olden times, the wells were often guarded or kept by a keeper; perhaps the ghost was once a keeper. Norman Adams included this tale in his book 'Haunted Scotland' published in 1998, and he writes that a white witch called Lily Grant once lived at Whitehills near the well and perhaps she was the ghost. *See 83 to 138.*

1991   11th April – A fire destroyed part of the warehouses at the closed Banff Distillery, Inverboyndie. *See 1824, 1863, 1877, 1932, 1941, 1983, 1985, and 1991.*

1992   The site of the Craig of Boyne Castle built *c1300* was listed as an Ancient Scheduled Monument. Grid Ref NJ616661.

1993   The granary at the corner of Low Shore and Seafield Street built *c1800* was converted to flats.

1993   The monument known as the Hills of Boyndie which lies 700m SW of the Mill of Boyndie was listed as a Scheduled Ancient Monument. The site was recognised as having important historical significance due to the barrows and enclosure comprising of a group of ring ditches and square enclosures of the later prehistoric or the early historic period. This site was possibly a settlement or a burial site, possibly of more than one period. Grid Ref NJ661635.

1994   The population of Whitehills was approx 1,200.

1996   25th August – The last service was held in St. Brandon's Church, Boyndie before it closed. The congregation moved to the Parish Church, Seafield Street, Whitehills. *See 1773.*

1996   Mrs Isobel M. Watt was appointed the first female Session Clerk in the history of the Church in the Parish of Boyndie.

Whitehills Parish Church, Seafield Street. (Isobel Watt).

1998   January - St. Brandon's Church at Boyndie with agreement with the congregation was sold by the Church of Scotland to Mr. and Mrs Whitehouse who converted it to an art gallery known as Art Caput. *See 1773, 1922, and 2000.*

1999   The Boyndie Trust was established. Registered Charity No. SCO29061.

1999   14th August - The coat of arms of Whitehills Community Council were officially granted. The arms were designed following a children's competition, and show a Scottish thistle, and wheat stalks (Symbols of agriculture) and an anchor and a fish (Symbols of fishing), these being the main economic activities in the area. The motto 'Heave Awa Fitehill's' is in Doric, and is said to be a fisherman's cry. Funds were raised by the Whitehills Millennium Committee.

Whitehills Community Council coat of arms.

1999 Banffshire Partnership Limited was established. Registered Charity No. SCO29693.

2000 14th February – Art Caput formerly St. Brandon's Church, Boyndie was gutted by fire. *See 1773, 1922, and 1998.*

2001 Whitehills Harbour was converted to a marina. The marina has forty serviced pontoon berths, plus seven un-serviced pontoon berths.

Whitehills Marina. (S. Bruce).

2001 Whitehills won the title of 'Scottish Community of the Year'.

2001 The Compass Rose, which is sited just east of Whitehills Harbour was built.

Compass Rose, Whitehills. (S. Bruce).

2002 Former staff of Ladysbridge Hospital published a book titled "Ladysbridge" – The Story of a Hospital 1865 – 2003.

2003 January - Ladysbridge Hospital closed down. At its peak between 1975 and 1985, it catered for 550 patients. In 2000, it only accommodated 120 patients.

2003 In 2003, Whitehills won the title 'Scottish Community of the Year' in a competition sponsored by Calor Gas.

2004 The Boyndie Visitor Centre was awarded four star visitor attraction status from the Scottish Tourist Board.

2004 15th May – The Boyndie Visitor Centre in the former Boyndie School was officially opened. On 11th November, it was visited by the Princess Royal, Princess Anne (b.1950). (This building from the mid 1980's was used as a day centre).

Boyndie Visitor Centre. (S. Bruce).

Inside there is a fine café, shop, and a display of RAF Banff memorabilia, which was added in **2007**. The grounds have nicely laid out paths, a pond, wooden sculptures, and a fountain. *See c1860.*

Pond at Boyndie Visitor Centre. (S. Bruce).

Old School Boyndie Visitor Centre sign. (A. Bruce).

2004   Whitehills Harbour won the Grampian Awards for Business Enterprise and the Alick Buchanan Smith Spirit of Enterprise Award.

2005   Architectural drawings were drawn up by Mantell Ritchie Architects, Banff, for conversion of the Whitehills Lifeboat Shed to a house. The conversion work was carried out during 2009/10.

Whitehills Lifeboat Shed and Fish Market 2005.
(S. Bruce).

2005   The Whitehills Fishmarket was used for the last time. Whitehills fishing boat BF156 'Budding Rose' the last fishing boat of the village (Except for small lobster boats) still to use the harbour landed her catch here for the last time. She later berthed in Macduff. Whitehills was the last place in Scotland where the fishermen sold their catch direct rather than through a fish merchant.

BF156 'Budding Rose'. (S. Bruce).

2005   St. Brandon's Church Hall in Seafield Street was completely renovated and renamed St. Brandon's Church Centre. *See* **1901**.

St. Brandon's sign. (A. Bruce).

2005   The Boyndie Wind Farm Co-op was established for the purpose of owning a share in the Boyndie Wind Farm located at Boyndie Aerodrome. This was the first such co-operative in Scotland and in **2006** locals were given the opportunity to invest in renewable energy.

2006   Seven windmills were erected at Boyndie Aerodrome by Falck Renewables, these were capable of generating 14MW of electricity, enough to supply 8,500 homes. 716 members of the Boyndie Wind Farm Co-op established in 2005 purchased a £750,000 stake in the wind farm. An eighth windmill was erected in **2009**.

Two of the eight wind turbines at Boyndie Windfarm. (S. Bruce).

2006   North East Fabricators Ltd, Inverboyndie, were the Seatrade Award Winner for their M.O.B. Recovery Cage.

2008   January - Inside the Boyndie Visitors Centre a small exhibition was added displaying items related to RAF Banff.
The RAF Banff Association have separate plans to restore some of the old airfield buildings creating another visitor centre.

2007/8 The old Ladysbridge Railway Station building, which had been used as the pavilion at the playing fields at Blackpots was removed and the Whitehills and District Playing Fields Association built a new pavilion. *See 1968.*

New Pavilion, Playing Field, Blackpots, Whitehills.
(S. Bruce).

2007/8 On the former site of Findlay's Gift Centre at Whitehills Harbour, which itself was converted from a former fish house, a block of flats was erected and named Morven View. Morven is the cone shaped hill behind Dunbeath in Caithness, which can be seen across the Moray Firth on a clear day.

Morven View, Whitehills. (S. Bruce).

Findlay's Gift Centre 2004. (S. Bruce).

2008 A book titled 'The Herring Lassies – Following the Herring' written by Rosemary Sanderson was published by the Banffshire Maritime and Heritage Association, ISBN 978-09547960-6-8. An appendix by Isobel Watt of Whitehills gave an interview with Margaret Ann Lovie (c1904 to 1998) also of Whitehills who was a gutting quine (Lassie) who followed the herring. This book was an instant best-seller for the Association.

The Herring Lassies book.

2008 A book titled 'A Separate Little War' ISBN 9781906502133 by Andrew D. Bird was published. The book tells the story of RAF Banff Coastal Command Strike Wing at the Boyndie Aerodrome.

2008 The RAF Banff Strike Wing Memorial Trust and the RAF Banff Association with funding from the National Lottery Awards For All published a DVD titled 'RAF Banff Strike Wing – Striking Hard & Sure'.

2009   November – An eighth turbine was erected at the Boyndie Wind
Farm.

To finish, in Inverboyndie Kirkyard we have a heraldic panel
dated *1738* showing the coat of arms of James Milne of Mill of
Boyndie. However, I could see no others in the Parish except for
this fine panel erected at No. 14 Braeheads. Another interesting
find is the original tip from the Parish Church spire.

Lawson coat-of-
arms   with
motto 'Leve Et
Relius'   which
means   'Arise
and   re-
illumine', (Rise
and shine).

No.14 Braeheads, Lawson coat of arms.
(S. Bruce).

Original tip of
the spire of the
Whitehills
Parish Church
when it stood in
Seafield Street,
Banff. The tip
was lost when
the church was
dismantled
1925/6,
however it was
found in 1969

Original tip from the Parish Church spire.
(S. Bruce).

by Mrs Argo the owner of Killkern a bungalow built on the
former site of the church Banff. It was given to Whitehills
Parish Church in 1981 and can be seen inside the church.

Conclusion

During my research for this book, I have come across several areas in and around the village where improvements or work could be done to save items of local heritage or provide information to visitors. Some of these are:

1) The empty barometer box of 1858 on the Low Shore could have a false barometer installed, similar to the one at Portgordon Harbour, aside this a plaque with historical information could be erected.

2) The Inverboyndie Kirk could do with an information panel erected. This panel could give details of the kirk, the Viking attack, which gave the nearby names of Swordanes, and Arrdanes, and information about Banff Distillery.

3) Boyne Castle made safe, and a path laid.

4) Boyne Castle doo-cot restored and re-roofed, and a path laid.

5) The old well at Inverboyndie could be saved.

6) One of the old unused buildings at the harbour could be developed into a heritage centre / tourist attraction. There is an old Zulu fishing boat the 'Hirta II' lying on a dry berth at Macduff, which could possibly be fixed-up and become an attraction. A kiln similar to one used in the former Blackpots Brick and Tile Works could be built and clay tiles and pipes made as a tourist attraction.

7) The handrails on the railway bridge at Inverboyndie are currently unsafe and need repaired.

8) An information panel re the lifeboats of Whitehills could be erected at the harbour.

9) An information panel erected at the Whitehills Parish War Memorial giving information on date unveiled / abbreviations / details of medals awarded to local men / local fishing boats, which served in the wars.

Locals with any ideas how to improve the village should contact Whitehills and District Community Council.

Acknowledgements
Isobel Watt, Whitehills, for many photographs, information, and for scrutinising my draft copy.
George Lovie, Whitehills, for the fishermen photograph on page 52.
Rev. Brian Hendrie for allowing me to take photographs inside Whitehills Parish Church.
Whitehills Harbour Master for information on the RNLI and the 'Nar'.
Ernest Leslie, Whitehills for a loan of the Ladysbridge book (See below).
Whitehills and District Community Council for their financial support.

References
The New Statistical Account (1842).
The Ordnance Gazetteer of Scotland (1895).
The Church and Churchyard of Boyndie by William Cramond A.M., Schoolmaster of Cullen (1886).
"Ladysbridge" – The Story of a Hospital, 1865 – 2003. (2002).

Local community websites:
www.banffshiremaritime.org.uk
www.webhistorian.co.uk (Banffshire Maritime section).
www.whitehillsanddistrict.co.uk
www.banffshirepartners.co.uk
www.boyndievisitorcentre.co.uk
www.whitehillsharbour.co.uk
www.whitehills.aberdeenshire.sch.uk

Appendix A
Scheduled Ancient Monuments in & around Whitehills.

Description	Date	Grid Ref
Hills of Boyndie, barrows & enclosures 700m SW of Mill of Boyndie.	Prehistoric.	NJ656638.
St. Brandan's Stone Circle.	Prehistoric.	NJ607610.
Boyne Castle.	c1580.	NJ611656.
Inverboyndie Kirk.	1634.	NJ666645.

Appendix B
Listed Buildings in & around Whitehills.

The following tables have been complied from the Historic Scotland database.

Listing categories

Buildings are assigned to one of three categories according to their relative importance. All listed buildings receive equal legal protection, and protection applies equally to the interior and exterior of all listed buildings regardless of category.

Category A - Buildings of national or international importance, either architectural or historic, or fine little-altered examples of some particular period, style or building type. (Approximately 8% of the total).

There are no Category A listed buildings in or around Whitehills.

Category B - Buildings of regional or more than local importance, or major examples of some particular period, style, or building type which may have been altered. (Approximately 51% of the total).

Category B building / address	Built	Date listed
Boyne Castle.	c1580.	22 Feb 72
Inverboyndie Kirk and burial ground.	c1634.	22 Feb 72
Boyne Castle, Doo-cot.	17th C.	23 May 90
Boyndie Parish Church, St. Brandon's. (Art Caput).	1773 with later additions.	22 Feb 72
Mains of Baldavie House.	Early-mid 18th century	23 May 90
Inverboyndie Bridge over the Burn of Boyndie.	Mid-late 18th century.	22 Feb 72

Appendix B
Listed Buildings in & around Whitehills (Continued).

Category B building / address	Built	Date listed
Seafield Arms Hotel, garden walls and gate piers, Chapel Street.	c1792/3 with later additions.	22 Feb 72
Bridge over the Burn of Boyne at Scotsmill.	Late 18th C.	23 May 90
Greystones, No. 22 Seafield Street and garden walls, Whitehills.	1794.	23 May 90
No. 9 Low Shore, Whitehills.	Early 19th C.	22 Feb 72
No. 1 Knock Street, Whitehills.	Early 19th C.	22 Feb 72
Girnal (Granary) / Warehouse Low Shore / Seafield Street.	c1800.	22 Feb 72
Bridge over the Burn of Boyne, Milton of Tillynaught.	c1800. (Collapsed Nov 2009).	15 Feb 82
No. 4 Low Shore, Whitehills.	c1800.	22 Feb 72
Stormcrest No. 17 Low Shore, Whitehills.	c1800.	22 Feb 72
Scotsmill Mill and former Steading.	Late 18th, early 19th C, possibly incorporating earlier fabric.	23 May 90
Mill of Boyndie Farmhouse.	1809 (Fronting 18th century building).	23 May 90
Knock House, No. 10 and 10A Knock Street, Whitehills.	1825.	22 Feb 72
Methodist Chapel, Chapel Street, Whitehills with enclosing walls and gate piers.	1840.	22 Feb 72
Church of Scotland Manse, Boyndie.	1841-2.	22 Feb 72
Ladysbridge Hospital, Troup Administration and Moor Newton Blocks.	1863-5.	23 May 90

Appendix B
Listed Buildings in & around Whitehills (Continued).

Category B building / address	Built	Date listed
No. 25 Low Shore, Whitehills.	1866.	22 Feb 72
Trinity Church (Church of Scotland), Seafield Street, Whitehills.	1879 / 1926.	22 Feb 72
Boyndie Parish Church (Church of Scotland), former Beadle's Cottage and Steading.	Late 19th century.	23 May 90
Lifeboat House and Slipway, Harbour Place, Whitehills.	1933.	23 May 90
Operations Block, Boyndie Airfield.	1942.	27 April 04
Control Tower, Boyndie Airfield.	1943.	27 April 04

Category C(S) – Buildings of local importance, lesser examples of any period, style, or building type, as originally constructed or moderately altered; and simple traditional buildings which group well with others in categories A and B. (Approximately 41% of the total).

There are far too many category C(S) listed buildings in Whitehills to list them all in this book, currently entered in the Historic Scotland register are 57 buildings.

Appendix C
Earls of Moray.

	Name	Born	Died	Earl dates	Succeeded by
1st	Thomas Randolph	-	1332	c1315 - 1332	His son.
2nd	Thomas Randolph[1]	-	1332	1332 - 1332	His brother.
3rd	John Randolph	1306	1346	1332 - 1346	His sister.
4th	Agnes Randolph[2]	c1312	1369	1346 - 1369	Extinct.

1) Thomas Randolph 2nd Earl held the title for only 23 days, he died at the Battle of Dupplin Moor (10th – 11th August 1332).
2) Agnes Randolph (Black Agnes of Dunbar) assumed the title of Countess of Moray.

Appendix D
Lairds of Boyne - Edmonstone's.

	Name	Born	Died	Laird dates	Succeeded by
1st	Sir John Edmonstone (Sir John de Edmunstone).	-	c1410	1369 - c1410	His son
2nd	Sir James Edmonstone	-	1486	c1410 – 1486	His son-in-law

Appendix E
Lairds of Boyne - Ogilvie's.

	Name	Born	Died	Laird dates	Succeeded by
1st	Sir Walter Ogilvie[1]	1460	1508	1486 - 1508	His son
2nd	Sir George Ogilvie	1480	1512	1508 - 1512	His son
3rd	Sir Walter Ogilvie	1504	1561	1512 - 1561	His son
4th	Sir Alexander Ogilvie	1530	1600	1561 – 1600	His son
5th	James Ogilvie	c1570	1619	1600 - 1619	His son
6th	Walter Ogilvie	-	1636	1619 - 1636	His son
7th	Sir Walter Ogilvie	-	1671	1636 - 1671	His son
8th	Sir Patrick Ogilvie[3]	-	1714	1666 - 1714	His son
9th	Sir James Ogilvie	1667	1727	1714 - 1727	Sold 1731[2]

1) Sir Walter Ogilvie (1460 to 1508) acquired the lands of Boyne in 1486 through marriage to Margaret Edmonstone, whom he married in 1484. She was the daughter and heir of Sir James Edmonstone (d.1486) 2nd Laird of Boyne.

2) In 1731 James Ogilvie sold Boyne Castle to his relative James Ogilvie (1688 to 1764) the 5th Earl of Findlater and 2nd Earl of Seafield

3) Sir Patrick Ogilvie (d.1714), Lord Boyne held the office of Lord of Session (Scotland). He was styled as Lord Boyne (Scottish Law Lord).

Appendix F
WW1 – Roll of Honour.

List of names on the Whitehills War Memorial, which is inscribed:
'To the greater glory of God and in memory of the men of the parish of Boyndie who made the supreme sacrifice in the Great War'.
(36 names). Dates from the Commonwealth War Graves Commission.

Rank	Name	Force	Date Died
Petty Officer	Francis Hendry	Royal Naval Reserve (T)	20/2/1916
Deck Hand	William Lovie	Royal Naval Reserve (T)	16/3/1917
Deck Hand	Francis Lawrence	Royal Naval Reserve (T)	16/3/1917
Deck Hand	Henry J. Ritchie	Royal Naval Reserve (T)	16/3/1917
Deck Hand	Alexander Ritchie	Royal Naval Reserve (T)	4/10/1916
Deck Hand	James H. Ritchie	Royal Naval Reserve (T)	15/2/1918
Deck Hand	James Ritchie	Royal Naval Reserve (T)	31/3/1917
Deck Hand	James Watson	Royal Naval Reserve (T)	16/3/1917
Seaman	Henry Ritchie	Royal Naval Reserve	13/12/1917
Sergeant	Robert Barbour	1st Gordon's	26/3/1918
Private	Henry G. Legge M.M.	1st Gordon's	23/10/1918
Private	Robert Buchan	2nd Gordon's	28/10/1914
Private	Frank Hepburn	2nd Gordon's	16/7/1918
Private	Alexander Lovie	2nd Gordon's	31/10/1914
Private	Alex B. Meldrum	4th Gordon's	20/9/1917
Corporal	James Morrison	6th Gordon's	10/2/1915
Private	John Robertson	6th Gordon's	25/9/1915
Private	Hugh Nicol	8th Gordon's	4/10/1915
Private	Alexander Merson	9th Gordon's	5/8/1917
Sergeant	Arthur Watson	8th Seaforth's	8/2/1918
Lance Corporal	George Ross	8th A&S Highlanders	14/9/1915
Private	James Cruickshank	8th A&S Highlanders	5/7/1917
Lance Corporal	George Stuart	Black Watch	17/11/1917
Private	George Wilson	2nd Scots Gds	26/9/1916
Private	Robert W. Spalding	9th Royal Scots	18/5/1916
Private	Alexander Urquhart	10th H.L.I.	19/11/1915
GNR.	George C. Allan	R.F.A.	5/10/1917
TRPR	Alexander A. Morrison	Household Battalion	12/10/1917
Rifleman	George Morrison	Rifle Brigade	2/9/1918

Appendix F
WW1 – Roll of Honour (Continued).

Rank	Name	Force	Date Died
Private	George McKenzie	9th Yorks Regiment	10/10/1918
Corporal	James Mitchell M.M.	M. G. Corps	29/5/1917
BMBDR	Alexander Nicol	Canadian F.A.	3/5/1917
Private	John Meldrum	19th Canadian Battalion	1/10/1916
Private	Alexander R. Barron	28th Canadian Battalion	6/6/1916
Private	Robert Esson	South African's	18/5/1916
Private	Robert Benzie	N. Z. Ex Force	28/9/1916

M.M. Military Medal awarded.

Appendix G
WW2 – Roll of Honour.

Names as shown on the Whitehills War Memorial. (15 names).
Dates from the Commonwealth War Graves Commission.

Rank	Name	Force	Date Died
Spec. Wrtr.	Charles Enwright	Royal Navy	6/7/1944
2nd Hand	George Lovie	Royal Navy	30/9/1941
A/B	James Watson	Royal Navy	10/11/1943
Seaman	William G. Mair	Royal Naval Reserve	11/4/1942
Sub- Lieutenant	David Milne	Royal Naval Volunteer Reserve	21/8/1944
Private	Jas. Chisholm	2nd Gordon's	27/12/1943
Private	Robert Innes	5 / 7th Gordon's	16/12/1944
Private	Alexander Shearer	5 / 7th Gordon's	16 or 17 /3/1943
Lieutenant-Colonel	Herbert J. Green	R.A.M.C.	27/12/1946
Sergeant Pilot	Victor Allison	R.A.F.	8/5/1940
Corporal	George Smith	R.A.F.	13/7/1942
A.C.I.	Alexander Gardiner	R.A.F.	4/9/1942
3rd Radio Officer	Samuel Watson	Merchant Navy	11/4/1945
Seaman	James L. Watson	Merchant Navy	29/10/1944
Seaman	James G. Watson	Merchant Navy	18/3/1943

Appendix H
War Memorial Abbreviations.

A/B	Able Seaman.
A.C.I.	Aircraftsman 1st Class.
A&S Highlanders	Argyll and Sutherland Highlanders.
BMBDR	Bombardier.
Canadian F.A.	Canadian Field Artillery.
GNR	Gunner.
H.L.I.	Highland Light Infantry.
M.G. Corps	Machine Gun Corps.
M.M.	Military Medal.
N.Z. Ex Force	New Zealand Expeditionary Force.
R.A.M.C.	Royal Army Medical Corps.
R.F.A.	Royal Field Artillery.
SCOTS GDS	Scots Guards.
Spec. Wrtr.	Specification Writer
TRPR	Trooper.

The New Road (Boyne Street), Whitehills. (Courtesy Isobel Watt).

Appendix I
Obituary to Herbert John Green,
From the British Medical Journal 8th February 1947.

"The death of Mr. HERBERT JOHN GREEN at the early age of 40 has cut short what appeared to be a career of great promise. Mr. Green was born at Boyndie in Banffshire, where his father was a successful farmer, and he was educated at Banff Academy. From there he passed to the University of Aberdeen and graduated M.B., Ch.B. in 1930. He was resident house-surgeon to the Aberdeen Royal Infirmary, and afterwards to the Royal National Orthopaedic Hospital London. In 1932, he settled in practice in Banff, and was early appointed to the staff of Chalmers Hospital. Here he carried out surgical work of high quality, and in 1937, he obtained F.R.C.S.Ed. Becoming interested in obstetrics and gynaecology, he gave up his practice when he was appointed to the Jessop Hospital for Women, Sheffield, in 1938. Here he worked hard and successfully, and in the following year was made registrar to the hospital and tutor in the department of obstetrics and gynaecology of Sheffield University. He obtained the M.R.C.O.G. in 1940. On the outbreak of war in 1939, Mr. Green was called on service as medical officer to the Banffshire R.A. Territorial Unit. He served throughout the war, at one time holding administrative staff appointments, but for the greater part of service, he held surgical appointments in India and Ceylon. He attained the rank of Liet.-colonel. Just over a year ago, Mr. Green was demobilized and took up again his appointment in Sheffield, where his interest in obstetrical and gynaecological work continued unabated. It seemed likely that he would worthily uphold the reputation of the Jessop Hospital in the future, but this was not to be. Mr. Green was tall, and had a genial disposition which brought him many friends both in Banff and Sheffield. He was held in high esteem by the board and the staff of the Jessop Hospital, and was popular among the students, who profited by his teaching. He was a careful and conscientious surgeon. He is survived by his wife and two sons".

Died 27th December 1946.

Appendix J
Whitehills RNLI Lifeboats.

Date	Name	Length	Breadth	Other Info
1924 - 1928	George and Mary Berrey	35'	8' 6"	No. 479 Self-righting
1928 - 1932	George Gordon Moir	35'	10'	No. 606 Self-righting
1932 - 1948	Civil Service No. 4	35' 6"	8' 10"	No. 756 Self-righting
1948 - 1949	William Maynard	40'	10' 6"	No. 746 Self-righting
1949 - 1952	Thomas Markby	40'	11' 8"	No. 706
1952 - 1960	St. Andrew (Civil Service No. 10)	41'	11' 8"	No. 897
1960 - 1961	Sarah Ward & William David Crossweller	45' 6"	12' 6"	No. 716
1961 - 1969	Helen Wycherley	47'	13'	No.959

Lifeboat crew of the St. Andrew (Civil Service No. 10), Whitehills.
(Photo courtesy Whitehills and District Community Council).

Other titles available from the
Banffshire Maritime & Heritage Association:

Along the Coast – Burghead to Portknockie (2010) by Stanley Bruce.
ISBN 978-1-907234-09-5.

Along The Coast – Cullen to Pennan 2nd edition (2010) by Stanley Bruce.
ISBN 978-1-907234-08-8.

Hall Russell Remembered – Shipbuilding in Aberdeen 1864 to 1992 (2009).
2nd edition by Stanley Bruce. ISBN 978-1-907234-02-6.

Coming Hame - Poetry Anthology (2009).
Edited by Stanley Bruce. ISBN 978-1-907234-01-9.

Back to the Sea – An Introduction to Peter Frederick Anson and his life on
the east coast of Scotland (2009).
By Stanley Bruce and Tina Harris. ISBN 978-1-907234-00-2.

Along the Coast – Pennan to St Fergus (2009).
By Stanley Bruce. ISBN 978-9547960-9-9.

Macduff Through the Years (2008).
By Stanley Bruce. ISBN 978-0-9547960-8-2.

The Herring Lassies – Following the Herring (2008).
By Rosemary Sanderson, edited by Stanley Bruce. ISBN 978-09547960-6-8.

Macduff Roll of Honour 1914 – 1919 (2008).
Edited by Stanley Bruce. ISBN 978-09547960-7-5. **SOLD OUT**

Along the Coast - Cullen to Pennan (2007).
By Stanley Bruce. ISBN 978-9547960-4-4. **SOLD OUT**

Coasting – Poetry Anthology (2007).
Edited by Stanley Bruce. ISBN 978-0-9547960-5-1.

Hall Russell Remembered (2007). By Stanley Bruce. **SOLD OUT**

Macduff Parish Church Bi-centenary (2005) (Revised and reprinted 2007).
By Stanley Bruce. **SOLD OUT**

Other titles by this author:

Fraserburgh Through the Years (2010). ISBN 978-1-907234-07-1.
Comforting Words (2006). ISBN 0-9547960-3-9.
Bard o Buchan Vol 1 (2005). ISBN 0-9547960-2-0.
The Bard o' the Broch (2004). ISBN 0-9547960-1-2. **SOLD OUT**
The Bard of Banff (2004). ISBN 0-9547960-0-4.